T0121796

POSING
For My
FATHER

POSING
For My
FATHER

A memoir

Mary Lee Gowland

iUniverse, Inc.
Bloomington

Posing For My Father
A memoir

Copyright © 2013 by Mary Lee Gowland.

All rights reserved. No part of this book may be used or reproduced by any means, graphic, electronic, or mechanical, including photocopying, recording, taping or by any information storage retrieval system without the written permission of the publisher except in the case of brief quotations embodied in critical articles and reviews.

iUniverse books may be ordered through booksellers or by contacting:

iUniverse
1663 Liberty Drive
Bloomington, IN 47403
www.iuniverse.com
1-800-Authors (1-800-288-4677)

Because of the dynamic nature of the Internet, any web addresses or links contained in this book may have changed since publication and may no longer be valid. The views expressed in this work are solely those of the author and do not necessarily reflect the views of the publisher, and the publisher hereby disclaims any responsibility for them.

Any people depicted in stock imagery provided by Thinkstock are models, and such images are being used for illustrative purposes only.
Certain stock imagery © Thinkstock.

ISBN: 978-1-4759-7563-5 (sc)
ISBN: 978-1-4759-7564-2 (hc)
ISBN: 978-1-4759-7565-9 (ebk)

Printed in the United States of America

iUniverse rev. date: 03/27/2013

Contents

Natural Light

my eight-year-old sister
sucks her thumb

I'm two
nestled beside her
sucking two fingers
and twirling my hair

mother reads to us
in our travel trailer

where's father?

behind the camera
telling us to pretend
it's night

because
morning light
streaming through
the Venetian blinds
is so much nicer
than using
a hot, harsh flash

Foreword

In high school I was known as the girl whose father took pictures of naked women. Boys wanted to hang out at my house, hoping to glimpse Peter Gowland photographing a *Playboy* centerfold. Or perhaps they'd get to see Jayne Mansfield or Raquel Welch or another Hollywood celebrity.

I didn't have an ordinary childhood. I grew up in the 1950s and 60s, in a home/studio with no separation between my parents' work and home life. If someone called during dinner, my father thought nothing of letting his food grow cold while he gave advice to one of his fans, or chatted with other professionals about the advantages of using his Gowlandflex cameras, which he designed and built in the garage.

My sister and I knew everything we did could be photographed and used in a book or magazine article. Most of the time it was fun to pose for his camera, as we did every year for our funny Christmas cards. But just as a photograph is made up of light and shadow, there was a dark side to being a photographer's daughter. Sometimes I wanted privacy and didn't like a house full of strangers.

In adolescence I wondered, would I be as beautiful as the people who surrounded me, not just models, but my parents as well? And when I fell in love, would my sweetheart be like my father, who needed more than one woman in his life?

Posing for My Father spans my first twenty years, up to the time my parents and I published *Tender Bough*, and I left L.A. Along the way I met many well-known people from Alfred Hitchcock to Charlie Manson. My diaries and hundreds of photographs have helped me relive and now share memories of that golden time.

Chapter 1

BEFORE I WAS BORN

My parents got married on their third date, December 21, 1941, as they liked to say "the longest night of the year."

Just a few weeks before, my mother, Alice Adams, had been a twenty-one-year-old, Sunday-school-teaching virgin, living with her parents, in Los Angeles. My father, Peter Gowland, had not had such a stable life.

Both his parents had left England to pursue acting careers in Canada. My eighteen-year-old grandmother had changed her name from Beatrice Bird to Sylvia Andrew. We always called her Andy.

My grandfather, Thomas Henry Gowland, became known as Gibson Gowland, Gibby to our family. Andy fell in love with the big, burly, thirty-six-year-old from Northumberland who had lived in South Africa, when she first saw him carrying a giant wooden cross down the aisle of the Anglican Church in Victoria, B.C. She mistook this to mean he was a religious man, but he just liked all those eyes upon him.

When she saw him again in an acting class, she convinced him they should go to Hollywood, where motion pictures were becoming a huge industry. Mary Pickford, Douglas Fairbanks, Clara Bow, Charlie Chaplin and Buster Keaton were some of the silent "movie stars" that captivated America.

Gibson and Andy hastily married and boarded a train south. When they mistakenly got off in San Francisco, they were told they had another 380 miles to go.

They found work right away as extras and character actors in such epics as D.W. Griffith's *Birth of a Nation* and *Intolerance*. They rented a small house in Ocean Park. After one miscarriage, my father Peter (after Peter Pan) was born, on April 3, 1916. The marriage didn't last. Andy, a sensitive poet and actress, could not tolerate the gruffness of the taciturn old bloke she married. They divorced when Peter was two.

I don't know why the judge awarded Gibson custody, with Andy having visitation rights. Against the court order, Gibson took five-year-old Peter with him when he got work on a movie filming in England, and didn't notify my grandmother. When she finally got Gibson's agent to spill the beans, she was furious. She took the train, then a ship, to England. When she located Gibson, she took Peter to her parents' house in London.

Andy's mother was one of the first women doctors in England, having gotten her degree in Ireland because women weren't admitted to English medical schools at the time. Her father was a physician as well, and a life-long vegetarian who donated his body to science. From their home they operated a small clinic.

Young Peter loved it there. He found medicine fascinating and adored his grandparents. Andy fell in love with Bernie Meakin, an Irishman, and they married in 1922 and moved to Los Angeles. That marriage didn't last long either. The only thing I know about him is that he was rumored to have been active in Sinn Féin, the Irish Nationalist movement.

In the meantime, Gibson returned to Hollywood with Peter in tow, and became a well-known character actor. His most famous role was McTeague in Eric von Stroheim's *Greed,* co-starring Zasu Pitts and Gene Herscholt. The eight-hour epic was shot in San Francisco and Death Valley, because von Stroheim wanted realism—real blisters, real sweat, real hardship. Peter stayed with neighbors who ran a nursery school called Baby Land. When Andy found ten-year-old Peter running around barefoot and covered in fleas she took Gibson to court. She wanted custody.

Instead the judge ordered Peter to boarding school. One night before bed, Gibson told Peter to pack his suitcase. In the morning he told him to pick his favorite toy—my father chose his red fire truck—and drove him to the Hollywood Military Academy. A man of few words, he simply told my father, "You have to live here now."

That night, Peter clutched his little truck and cried himself to sleep. He used to say, "That was the last time I cried."

But, after a few weeks, Peter grew to like the military academy. He had three hot meals a day, in contrast to the canned beans his father had often served for dinner. He had never worn shiny shoes and a uniform before. He made friends, including Bill Reid whose father was the famous movie heartthrob, Wallace Reid.

Peter probably would have been happy there a long time, but Gibson squandered his earnings from *Greed* and could no longer afford the tuition. Peter went back to live with his father in the $15.00-a-month shack on Pacific Coast Highway in Malibu and commuted to school in Santa Monica, as there were no schools in Malibu at that time.

Peter liked the beach and got an Airedale terrier he named Puppy. For his fifteenth birthday, Gibson bought him a Brownie camera. Peter loved taking pictures and was good at it. Handsome and witty, he liked to take pictures of his friends, especially pretty girls, and never lacked for girlfriends. Life seemed perfect.

But then his dog got killed by a car and Gibson got work on movies that shot on location. During a school break, Peter accompanied his dad to Florida. When he got tonsillitis his dad checked him into a local hospital, where at age fourteen, he lost his virginity, to a pretty nurse.

Back in California, he got his driver license at fifteen, and drove himself to Hollywood High School where two of his classmates were Judy Garland and Mickey Rooney. Eventually he moved in with his mom, in her Hollywood apartment, so he could be closer to school.

Andy's career hadn't been as lucrative as Gibson's. She got small parts and sold occasional stories and articles to magazines. She had an interest in spirituality and wrote poems. I inherited her copies of Kahlil Gibran's *The Prophet*, and Yogananda's *Autobiography of a Yogi*.

With the invention of "talkies," Gibson had trouble getting work because of his thick Northumberland accent. So he returned to England where he continued to work in films and married his second wife, who like my grandmother, was also eighteen years younger than him.

After high school Peter worked as a "dress extra," playing dashing soldiers and charming nineteenth-century gentlemen. He rented a small house on Barton Avenue in Los Angeles, and set up a studio and darkroom where he could develop and print the pictures he took in his spare time.

My mother had a more traditional upbringing. She was born in Pittsburgh, in 1920, to parents who hadn't married for love, or ambition.

Her mother almost married a professional baseball player. But she told him she didn't want to be married to someone who could be traded, like cattle. She hoped he'd change careers. But instead he broke their engagement. By the time she met my grandfather, she was a twenty-nine-year old spinster who had pretty much given up on getting married.

But Frank Adams was a nice guy who had also had his share of heartache. Together they settled into a comfortable, if not romantic marriage. My mother Alice was born on April 16, 1920, a year after her brother Ted, and a year before her brother Don.

In 1928 the family moved to California to be near my grandmother's favorite sister, Annie, who had married well.

Alice loved her parents and her brothers. She remembers her childhood as happy. As a teenager she loved attending Christian camp in the mountains above Los Angeles. She graduated from high school in 1938, got a job as a secretary and taught Sunday school.

The first week in December, 1941, Alice's boyfriend Johnny Block, asked her if she'd like to have her picture taken, by a friend of his. She said sure.

When she entered Peter's immaculate little bungalow Alice saw he had been sewing a cover for a speaker cabinet he had built. (I still have that old Singer sewing machine.) A corner of his living room was set up as a studio, complete with professional lights, camera stand, mirror and background.

He had also built a little tropical tiki bar out of bamboo, and planters along the windows for houseplants. He had upholstered old couches in sleek modern fabric, and built light sconces on the walls. Alice was impressed.

Peter and Alice's boyfriend Johnny looked like they could be brothers. Both were over six-feet tall with wavy brown hair. Alice was only five-foot-two. One of the first things Peter said to her that night was "If we ever have children, they'll be the perfect height."

Peter adjusted the lights and asked Alice to lie on her stomach on a fur-covered chaise lounge. She was reluctant to pull down her blouse and expose her shoulder, but eventually she relented. That night she found it hard to fall asleep, thinking of the handsome photographer with the sparkling blue eyes and tidy little home.

And Peter couldn't get her out of his mind either. He was a twenty-five-year old bachelor who had photographed dozens of beautiful women but had never been quite so smitten.

The next morning, he developed and printed the pictures he'd taken of Alice. Was it his expert lighting that made her appear so radiant? All he knew when he looked at her face was that he was in love.

That Sunday the horrible news that Pearl Harbor had been bombed was all over the radio. Alice's first, irrational impulse was to call Peter, not her boyfriend Johnny.

"I'm so scared," she said, "Can you come over?"

"I'm washing my car," he answered, "but if you want to come over here, you can."

She took the Red Line trolley. They consider this their first date. On their second date they went to a movie and had dessert at Queen Anne's Tea Room. Their third date fell on the winter solstice, December 21.

"Bring a coat," Peter told her on the phone.

"But it's warm out," she said.

"Just bring a coat," he said.

When he arrived, he asked if he could meet her mother, but Grandma would not come out because her hair was in curlers. When they got outside Alice saw another couple in the back seat of Peter's car. Alice introduced herself and the girl in the back seat began to giggle.

"Well, ask her!" the young woman she said to Peter.

"Ask me what?" Alice wanted to know.

"Do you want to get married tonight?" Peter asked.

"Sure," she answered with no hesitation.

Peter stopped at a pay phone, called Grandma and asked if he could take her daughter to Las Vegas and get married.

My grandmother said, "She's twenty-one, she can do what she wants."

After the wedding at The Hitching Post, the two couples drove back to Los Angeles. Peter dropped off his friends and took Alice directly to his house. She had no idea what lay ahead. The country was at war. They could all be killed any day. But wasn't it better to die in the arms of a handsome, handy photographer who loved her?

The next morning they went out to breakfast. Alice was floating on air. They gazed at each other across the table. Then, with a serious look on his face Peter said "What have we done?"

"We got married, silly!" she responded, too star-struck to see the misgiving in his eyes.

Not long after, she came home from work one afternoon and heard giggles. She found Peter in the darkroom with a pretty brunette. Both had guilty looks on their faces.

She immediately left the room and locked herself in the bedroom, expecting Peter to knock on the door and assure her there was nothing to worry about. But no knock came. She felt like a fool. But there was no way she was going to let anyone know about this. She was married. For better or worse. Period.

My sister Ann was born the following December, 1942. When the war ended, Ann was two-and-a-half. Peter got drafted and sent to Germany, for The Occupation. He always said this was one of the happiest times of his life. The war was over. He was twenty-eight. His wife and daughter were safe, having moved in with her parents. He enjoyed his time as a military photographer, documenting not only ruin and rubble but beautiful winter landscapes and saucy German *frauleins*.

Alice worked at night, as a waitress at The Drunkard restaurant that had musical entertainment. She saved all her pay checks and my dad's military salary and when he returned, with the help of the GI Bill, they built their first home/studio on Overland Avenue, a busy commercial street, just south of Olympic Boulevard, in West Los Angeles.

With my mother's keen business sense and my father's photographic skills, Peter was able to quit his day job and devote himself fulltime to taking pictures. My mother loved to write, so she took the information he dictated and turned it into interesting articles and eventually books.

I was born in Queen of Angels Hospital on May 6, 1949.

Season's Greetings

Chapter 2

OVERLAND AVENUE

I liked growing up in a business. At night the rhythmic tap of my mother's Royal typewriter lulled me to sleep. I liked to watch my father set up lights in the studio and unfurl gigantic rolls of thick, colored paper down the wall as a background. I liked meeting models who came to have their pictures taken. They were pretty, they were nice to me.

When I was three, my mother started a folder of "Mary Lee's Sayings."

> Peter was photographing a pin-up model in the studio. The girl was lying on her stomach in a sheer negligee. The gown was pulled back to reveal part of

her hind-quarter. Mary Lee roamed into the studio and looked over the situation then said, "Your behind's uncovered." This remark sent the model and Peter into hysterics but Mary Lee was insistent, "Really," she said in a very serious voice, "really."

I like how Mother said I "roamed" into the studio, because that's how I remember it—roaming around the house until I found something that interested me.

Sometimes I would stand on the front stoop and watch cars drive by on the busy street. In summer I liked to sit in my wading pool for hours, observing. When Ringling Brothers Circus came to town, Mother walked me and my sister to the vacant lot where they'd set up their big tent. I loved the elephants, horses and big cats but was afraid of clowns with their scary painted faces. Perhaps it was after attending the circus that my father added to my sayings:

Feb 53 Mary Lee looking dejected. I asked what is the matter. She replied, "Daddy, I wanted to be a lion and they made me a people."

Peter Gowland Photography opened into a reception area. Along the right wall my father built a shoulder-high planter where Mother-in-Law Tongues grew. Two modern woven chairs were perpendicular to Mother's desk with its heavy black telephone and her big grey typewriter. Here she made calls to magazines and newspapers, asking if they would be interested in an article or photo spread. In a few short years their business grew and they were constantly busy.

During the day, the studio, with its wall of windows, was filled with natural light. My father, who became known for his flattering lighting, supplemented daylight with various forms of flash—bounce, strobe, fill-in, which were mounted on roll-around stands.

A short hallway with a darkroom on one side, bathroom and bedroom on the other, led to the kitchen and living room which had a brick fireplace, armless chairs and my parents' bed. My sister Ann and I shared the small bedroom until I was three and she was nine. Then it was converted into a full office that included a light box to view color transparencies, file cabinets, drawers of negatives and a work table.

Part of the garage was converted into a room for Ann. Mother often scolded her for leaving her shoes in her room and getting her socks dirty, walking through the patio to the house. I remember being curious about what Ann did out there, away from our parents' watchful eyes.

For me, a corner of the patio was enclosed by two glass walls. One day when I didn't feel well, one of my friends came over and stared in at me. There were no curtains to close, so I burrowed under the covers to hide. The floor was brick with a drain in the middle. I felt like I was living outside with no walls. I didn't like it.

I inherited Ann's hand-me-down doll, Noma, who had rubber legs and a loose big toe. I loved to wiggle that toe and peer at the white cloth stuffing inside her leg. I also had a toy panda whose red tongue I cut off. Why would a panda go around with his tongue hanging out?

Having a sister six-and-a-half years older often felt like I lived with three grownups. One night, when I was still sleeping in a crib, the bottom of the crib crashed to the floor. At my wails my parents came running. I remember looking up to see my mother, father and sister, with their hands on the side of the crib, looking down at me. I'm surprised there's no picture of this, as nearly everything else in my life was photographed: the day I was born, my first steps, my first birthday party and all the parties thereafter, all the Christmases when we had to wait until bright lights were set up before we could open our presents.

I got used to the lights and the cameras. They were like part of the family. I liked to pose and make my parents laugh. It was fun to try on hats before a mirror, hug a puppy, pet a kitten. In one of my favorite pictures, I'm not yet two, standing with my back to the camera, completely naked. I have one hand on my hip and the other on a tiny table with a bowl of fruit. One toe is pointed toward an empty picture frame on the floor. I'm sure my mother staged the picture. I'm not including it in this book because sadly, in this day and age it might be considered inappropriate or worse. But in 1951 it had a sweet innocence.

My father often used the alley behind the house as an extension of his garage-workshop. I loved to watch him build furniture and sets. I loved the smell of sawdust. I loved to watch him use his shiny tools and how organized and neat he was. All his nails, screws and washers were lined up in jam jars on shelves above his work bench. His hammers, pliers, wrenches and coiled extension cords hung from a wall-mounted peg board.

Some of the first articles Mother sold to magazines were of my father's building projects, broken down and photographed, step-by-step. He created a beautiful playhouse for Ann, red with white scallop trim. *Better Homes & Gardens* turned the article into a booklet they gave to new subscribers. I learned from an early age that work should be fun. My parents philosophy was do what you love and money will follow.

Before I was born Ann was their star model. She was a beautiful child with big blue eyes. She was gregarious and outgoing, a natural actress. She played Spencer Tracy and Katherine Hepburn's daughter in *Sea of Grass* when she was three-years-old.

When Ann was four she auditioned for another part and got a call back. But the day before she was supposed to go, Mother was on the phone and told Ann not to go outside. But Ann disobeyed. She got on her tricycle and asked her friend to get on the back and push her. I guess her friend got going too fast, because Ann got scared and tried to stop. Her foot got caught in the spokes. She flew off and broke her leg. That was the end of Ann's movie career.

During my Overland Avenue years, Ann was at her most enterprising. She set up a little store on the sidewalk in front of the house. In the garage, she hung a sheet and put on a talent show starring neighborhood kids. My parents encouraged and photographed all her projects.

Whereas I liked dressing up and posing, Ann was a natural organizer. She always had some sort of project going where she could enlist her friends. I remember one day my parents were gone, probably at the beach or a park taking pictures. Ann and her friends dragged the pale birch-colored upright piano out into the patio and scraped off all the veneer.

"Don't tell!" she said to me, as if they wouldn't find out. I think my father was too angry to photograph that episode.

My mother was the disciplinarian in the family. My father was pretty easy going and hated confrontations. There are only a handful of times I remember him losing his temper. Once was when Ann had done something to upset me. I ran into his studio and tattled.

"Ann's being mean!" I wailed.

Without a word, he walked into the kitchen and punched her in the back. I felt terrible. I never thought he would strike either one of us. I just wanted him to tell her to stop being mean to me. Immediately I was filled with remorse—I feel bad about it to this day. But also, I was shocked to see this side of my easy-going father. My stomach hurt knowing the man I loved and trusted most in the world could be violent.

My mother was more apt to raise her voice when she had "had it up to here" with me, my sister or my dad. But she also got over her anger quickly. Once it was out, it was gone. But one day, when I was three, my father did something that so upset her she said she was leaving him.

"Get in the car!" she commanded me and my sister.

Ann said, "No!" but I obeyed, grabbing my tongue-less panda.

I remember sitting in the front seat of our 1953 Chevy as we drove through the dark night, up into the hills. We spent the night at the Beverly Hills Hotel.

I didn't like being taken away from my house. But once we arrived and I got out of the car, I breathed in the delicious fragrance of big trees and wide lawns. We didn't have any of this on Overland Avenue. Our backyard was a brick patio between the house and garage and our front yard was the street. The only greenery I knew was our neighbor's hedge, on the other side of the alley.

The lush canyon was wonderful. I heard birds and saw a bushy-tailed squirrel. The music of frogs croaking and crickets chirping was even better than the sound of mother typing. I snuggled into the comfy bed next to my sad mother and fell asleep.

We went home in the morning and things returned to normal for a while. Models came and went. The phone rang. Ann played with her friends. Daddy took pictures. Mommy typed and cooked dinner. When it was warm enough, Mommy and Daddy carried the dinner table into the patio, and Daddy cooked spareribs or hamburgers in the brick barbecue he had built.

One night I dreamed that I could see all of us eating our dinner. It was as if I were above, looking down. I saw the white table cloth and the clear glass bottle of Adohr milk. (Adhor was Rhoda backwards, the name of the milk company owner's daughter.) I saw the ceramic pot of baked beans. I saw the tops of our heads. I couldn't hear us talking, so it was like watching a silent movie.

In the morning I ran out to the patio and looked up. I expected to see lattice work or something that I could have climbed up on to get that point of view. But there was nothing up there. This was troubling, yet strangely intriguing. How did I see it? What were dreams anyway?

I gazed into the black, button eyes of my stuffed-sock monkey, but found no answer there. I dropped him on the floor and stuck two fingers in my mouth. With my other hand I twirled a lock of hair.

When I wasn't watching my parents work, I liked to watch television. My first crush was Sheriff John, on Channel 11. *Sheriff John's Lunch Brigade* debuted in 1949, the year I was born. When I was three it won an Emmy for Outstanding Children's Program. Sheriff John started the show by singing, "Laugh and be happy, and the world will laugh with you . . ." and closed with "Aloha, adios, adieu, God bless you," which may have inspired my interest in foreign languages.

Sheriff John showed cartoons, which I didn't particularly enjoy. I couldn't find anything to like about Porky Pig or Crusader Rabbit. But I did like how Sheriff John taught us about safety and manners, and we always said the Pledge of Allegiance. Kids could send in their birth dates and Sheriff John would sing the Birthday Polka to them. I believe my love of poetry came from lines like, "a song will make a hat rack look like a Christmas tree."

Engineer Bill was on Channel 9. But how can a train engineer compete with a sheriff? He did play a game with us that I liked: Red Light, Green Light. We were told to ask our mother to get us a glass of milk. Then when he said "green light" we'd drink and when he said "red light" we'd stop—without spilling! I liked this challenge.

I developed an appreciation for TV at an early age, cuddling with my parents on their bed in the living room watching adult shows. *Milton Berle* and his great cast had us in stitches. I liked *The Honeymooners,* set in the tiny kitchen of New York bus driver Ralph Cramden and his wife Alice. When he got exasperated with her he'd threaten: "A trip to the moon Alice!" and we'd all laugh. *Ted Mack's Amateur Hour,* a forerunner of American Idol had lots of great acts. We loved to guess the answers on *You Bet Your Life* with Groucho Marx or the more serious *Sixty-Four Thousand Dollar Question. Playhouse 90* offered live dramas that made us feel we were right there in the theater.

Once, crawling around my mother, I accidentally poked her with my elbow. She grabbed her breast and told me to be more careful. Sometime afterwards she had a small lump removed. I blamed myself. I thought I had given my mother cancer, but thankfully it was not malignant. For years her one-inch scar would not let me forget that we sometimes hurt each other without meaning to.

One rainy night my father heard a faint mewing outside. He opened the front door and a little black kitten ran into the house, dashed down the hall and hid under my parents' bed. I laid on the carpet and peered into two bright, frightened yellow eyes. I knew right away that it would be mine. I didn't care if it was a boy or a girl. We were alike. We were both young and small and remember, I wanted to be born a lion. We named him Humphrey after Humphrey Bogart. Another cat that came to us on Overland was black-and-white. He was called Fearless Fosdick, like a character in the Dick Tracy comics.

Because my parents set their own work schedule, we were able to take many trips in our travel trailer. I was assigned to the top bunk right under the sloping roof. I'd hit my head when I'd sit up. In the night if I had to go to the bathroom, I'd crawl down and pee in a ceramic pot to avoid a long hike through dark, scary campgrounds.

Looking at photos of a trip to the mountains, I wonder if my father really caught that trout he's frying over an open fire, or did we bring it with us from Santa Monica? Maybe Mother caught it. After all, she had loved camping with her fellow Christians when she was a teenager.

Photographs from our trip to the Petrified Forest are in the chapter "Continuity" in *How to Take Better Home Movies,* published in 1956, although we had taken the trip in 1953. Here's what my mother recorded:

> When we were getting ready to take a trip to Arizona in our trailer, we wanted the girls to enjoy it so kept talking about the different things we'd see. One thing we kept mentioning was the fact that we'd see lots of Indians. When we were at last on our way, driving a particularly long stretch of road, Mary Lee had been thinking very quietly and she suddenly asked, "Mommy, do Indians have tongues?"

My question made perfect sense to me because I'd seen how Indians were depicted in movies and on TV. They grunted "How" but not much else.

A consequence of living in an environment of constant activity and stimulation was that when it came time to send me to nursery school I didn't want to go. What would I miss when I was gone? Plus, the little school had a depressing fenced-in asphalt yard that I hated. It felt like being in a cage. If both my parents were busy, our maid Bea, who came twice a week to clean and iron, would take me by the hand and march me down the block.

I didn't like having to sit on the floor with a bunch of little kids and sing songs like "Itsy Bitsy Spider." I wanted to stay home where I could dress up, dance, sit on my father's lap and watch him feed rolls of film into his black metal cameras. I wanted to watch my mother help a model with her makeup, and pose her, and arrange her clothes.

Chapter 3

RUSTIC CANYON

My father learned about Rustic Canyon from Bill Reid, his old buddy from Hollywood Military Academy. Both the boys' fathers were actors. But whereas Peter's father was a character actor, and English at that, Bill's father was William Wallace Reid, who had been called "the screens most perfect lover." Sadly he died in 1923 when Bill was only six.

By the time my father was a successful photographer, Bill and his family were living a quarter of a mile from Will Rogers State Beach, on Lower Amalfi Drive, near Canyon Elementary School. Bill told my father that lots were opening up in Rustic Canyon, further up the hill.

Narrow, winding Mesa Road leads up to Rustic Canyon. It's reminiscent of the south of France, with houses crammed close together on steep lots. But once you reach Latimer Road everything opens up. Large parcels have houses set back from the street. Many of the homes are hidden by an overgrowth of trees, flowering shrubs and tropical plants—elephant ears, pampas grass, bougainvillea, morning glory, and honeysuckle. Trickling springs leak into the streets creating paths of green moss. A year-round creek flows from the Santa Monica Mountains all the way to the beach.

In the 1920s the agriculture department at UCLA planted lots of trees and non-native shrubs. Sycamores and many varieties of pine would eventually dwarf the native oaks. A protected grove of shaggy-barked eucalyptus stands next to Rustic Canyon Park filling the air with the pungent smell of camphor.

By the time my parents explored the canyon in 1954, new ranch-style homes were sprouting up alongside original log cabins of the 1920s. I always assumed the nickname "Uplifters Ranch" which hangs on a wooden sign over the street at the entrance to the park, had something to do with benevolence. But it was named by a group of Hollywood actors, who "uplifted" their glasses of whisky and rum, thumbing their noses at Prohibition.

THE CREEK

The creek cut through disintegrating granite
on its way from the Santa Monica mountains
to its eventual demise at the shore. What was it called
that creek that ran through my childhood, that trickled
placidly in summer, full of watercress and pollywogs
and roared in muddy anger in January, spitting
and slicing at the roots of young trees?

My parents had to pick their way through the icy stream
that day they came to survey the lot. I can see my mother
in pedal pushers, her tan legs freshly shaved,
toenails painted red. She carried her sandals daintily
as my father forged ahead, khaki trousers rolled.
They were young, handsome, vulnerable and in awe,
seeing their dream as raw land, wild and overgrown.

Everything was scruffy and dry. It was August.
Poison oak was turning red. But they envisioned
in that small parcel a wooden bridge, paved driveway,
and a wide open house where people would come,
in spite of it being so far away from any place they had ever known.
It might as well have been on Mars. There were no sidewalks,
no streetlights. At night sounds of crickets and coyotes mingled
with the gurgle of the creek. It was fun, it was frightening,
to consider the distance from the city, from their pasts.

And we, their children, what was this new home to us,
who had lived on Overland Avenue where trucks rumbled by?
My sister was twelve, already interested in boys,
who would jump off our roof into the pool, guys with
Pachuco hair, all greased up. My memory of Ann is vague.
Her presence like a boarder who had more important things to do.
By the time I was twelve she had moved into a stucco apartment
and her room, the *good* room, that overlooked the creek, became mine.

I remember thick black mud, how it oozed when we stuck it,
the tangle of stinging nettles along the bank, clumps of dark green
watercress and water so icy our fingers turned red.
We made Inca villages and played that we were *señoritas*
in Spanish California. And when we were fourteen,
the creek was our path to the beach, a mile away.
Far from the house it became a concrete storm drain
flat, gray, slippery with slimy moss and littered with beer cans.
The wild banks were replaced by prison-like walls topped with
chain-link fence. And all that pristine water, which had once
been melting snow, sat stagnant in lukewarm pools. Finally
it ended in what we called the Polio Pond, a warm murky lake
the ocean lapped at, the way wild animals clean each other.
That piss-warm pond was perfect for adolescents
to build island forts and worry our parents.

Our magic lagoon, full of mystery and potential, was dwarfed
by the ocean whose constant, impersonal breaking of waves
followed us all the way home, as we ambled back up the stream
sunburned and salty, past dog-do and people's trash.
The roar was still audible when we entered again
the comforting familiarity of sumac and oak. That
slate gray ocean could still be heard, pounding dolefully.
Its loneliness seemed to crave the security and seclusion
of a canyon creek. Was the ocean jealous of our salt-free,
tree-lined little river, that flowed so congenially through our lives?

Bill Reid designed and constructed the wooden bridge over the
creek. Once it was completed two homes were built: the Vos' small
ranch-style house, and my parents ultra modern "contemporary"
designed by Bill Overpeck, a young architect who designed the
round hotel towers in Marina del Rey.

For the year that our new home was being built, we rented a
little yellow house at 11 Latimer Road. I was alarmed, at the age
of five, to realize it didn't have a chimney for Santa Claus to come
down. My mother assured me that he would figure out how to get
inside. He could come in the kitchen door, like we did, or walk
around to the patio and open the sliding glass door.

After living so long on a busy thoroughfare I was a little afraid
in the shady canyon. Nights were pitch black. Next door was a very
dark, brown house, owned by a pallid hermit who frightened me
whenever I happened to get a look at him. One night he shot off a
gun. My parents called the police. I was so scared I threw up.

I started lip-syncing when I lived on Latimer Road. Mother
dressed me in a navy blue silk slip, all pinned in the back, pearls,
earrings and gold "mules." She draped a white rabbit stole around
my shoulders and put "Let Me Go Lover" by Patti Page on the
turntable. One of the photos became our Christmas card on which
Mother hand wrote, "Auld Lang Syne."

Living just a block away from our new house meant we could
watch the progress on a daily basis. What seemed like miles of shiny

copper pipe, for radiant heating, were laid before terrazzo was poured over it. Space was left for three in-ground planters. The long, low house had walls of thick plate glass facing the backyard which had a small swimming pool and a gray brick wall behind it. For several years a trickling waterfall coursed down the hill and spilled into the pool. Five steps led up to the Japanese inspired hillside.

Over time, the bamboo ground-cover choked out every other living thing until voracious ivy overtook it. But in the beginning, the design was pretty and serene. We dove from the steps into the deep end of the pool. Slate stepping stones led up the hillside past camellia bushes and low lights shining on three boulders. A brick landing opened up into a narrow canyon shaded by our neighbor's five-hundred-year-old oak tree. At the top of the hill, beyond sight, was the backyard of a house on Chautauqua Boulevard.

In the 1950s and '60s Rod Serling, James Arness, James Whitmore, Teresa Wright, Lloyd Bochner and Lee Marvin were our neighbors. In fact, most of the residents were in the entertainment business, whether actors, directors or lawyers. So my photographer parents fit right in.

When Tab Hunter and Rock Hudson came to have their pictures taken, they signed my autograph book. Raquel Welch was one of the first models to appear on the annual Rigid Tool calendar which was one of my parents' steady jobs.

Jayne Mansfield was kind and down to earth. I loved watching her body-builder husband, Mickey Hargitay lift her over his head as if she weighed nothing. Julie Newmar who played Stupifyin' Jones in the movie *Lil Abner*, would go on to be Cat Woman on the Batman TV show. She was charming and funny, a great dancer with incredibly high kicks, as was Mary Tyler Moore.

Alfred Hitchcock would not come to our house for a photo shoot commissioned by a magazine. My parents took me with them to his Brentwood home. I remember him being a serious little man in a gray suit. I was told to stay in his den where I could eat peanuts out of a plastic dispenser decorated with rhinestones, and play with his little white Sealyham terrier.

Rustic Canyon is still a hidden treasure. But very few of the original houses remain as they were. Where once there were lawns and front yards, many of the properties now are surrounded by high walls or contain a house so big there is no yard at all. There is still a sweetness to the air, of ocean and flowering ginger. But the quiet streets where young boys and girls rode bikes are now clogged with SUVs, gardeners' trucks, and cars belonging to people playing tennis at Rustic Canyon Park.

In my memory the streets are nearly empty. Sky is visible through trees that have not yet grown so big they choke out the sky. In my memory we knew all the neighbors by name.

Chapter 4

DAISIES

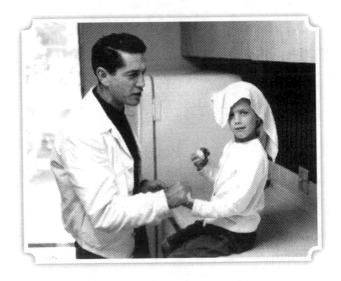

The sun cast shadows over the long, low house and blazed on towering sycamores across the creek. In my father's high-ceilinged photo studio with its thick glass wall opening into the backyard, my pretty mother knelt before me, pinned two artificial daisies on a black ribbon, and tied it around my six-year-old chest.

"We're going to do a dance for Daddy," she told me, "We're going to surprise him, pretend to be strippers, because he photographed a stripper today."

"What's a stripper?" I asked.

Mommy paused, taking a straight pin out of her mouth. "Well, they're . . . performers. Dancers! They're ladies who . . . dance."

"Like the June Taylor dancers on TV?" I asked.

"Yes, like the June Taylor dancers," she answered, smiling up at me.

"I'm going to try *this* one," Ann said, coming out of the dressing room. She showed us a blue bikini with a strapless top. At twelve, she already had a figure and was as tall as Mommy, who wore a fringed bikini she had made. She made most of the outfits models wore on calendars and magazine covers.

I was barefoot. Ann wore black high heels with ankle straps, and Mommy had on her gold-and-black mules. Both of them had short hair that Mommy called, "dishwater blond." My blond hair was cut in a Buster Brown—straight-across bangs and cropped at my chin. I had lost one of my front teeth.

When Ann came back out in the dark-blue bikini, we saw that it *did* fit. I loved the sound of her high heels clicking on the floor as she joined us in front of the mirror.

Satisfied with my make-shift bra, Mommy opened a hidden door in the wall and turned on the record player. There was a hiss before Peggy Lee's husky voice began: "You give me fev-a, fev-a in the mornin', fev-a all through the night."

We formed a line, watching ourselves in the big roll-around mirror and, as the day grew dimmer, in the wall of glass. Out in the yard I could see my black cat Humphrey watching us, crouched on the wall above the pool.

Mommy moved gracefully, like a real dancer. She had good timing and could remember steps she saw on TV. Ann and I followed as best we could, copying her as she extended her arms, bent her knees, turned, kicked and flicked a pink scarf.

While my sister and mother were perfectly at ease in their bikinis I struggled in my underpants, trying to hold up the ribbon that would slip down when I lifted my arms. I wondered: if Daddy liked the dance, would we do it at their next party? Mommy said the new house was perfect for parties and already they had put on a political fundraiser, had the neighbors over, and at Christmas they invited their friends from State Beach, which included many bachelors.

Ah, the bachelors. The men who would never marry. They fascinated me. Tan and muscular, they replaced the grandfathers I never knew: Freddie Zendar was a cinematographer. Steve Carruthers was a dress extra who looked like David Niven. My favorite, Joe

Gray, was a character actor and stunt man who often doubled for
Dean Martin.

SAVE-A-PLATE

One by one the men who never marry
show up on Sunday just at dusk
just as mother is putting potatoes on the table
just as father is taking steaks off the grill.
We hear a car and stop. My 16 year-old sister rolls her eyes.
It's bad enough to have to sit down together without this intrusion.

"Oh dear," mother says.

The doorbell chimes through the wide breezy house
into the yard, over the pool, bamboo, camellias.

It echoes over ivy and poison oak
and settles in the thick gray boughs of gnarly, old oaks.

My mother runs her fingers through her short blond hair,
walks across terrazzo in her shorts and rubber thongs.
She opens the door with a smile.

The men who never marry say,
"Oh, were you just about to eat?"

We feel their embarrassment
unable to hide their hunger
for a family
as they shuffle in, tan, sandy
from their long weekend at the beach.

My father says, "How about a snort?"
and pours a shot of dark amber over ice.

Steve Carruthers, debonair movie extra
with trim gray moustache.
Cecil Ballerino, who invented
"roll-on" mascara, who my mean sister says
is my real father. And
Joe "Save-a-plate" Gray,
Dean Martin's double
in his white '57 T-Bird, who told me,
"Don't make a move till you hear from me."

He was going to be my agent.
He was going to make me a star.

The men who never marry bring the scent
of seaweed and cigars into my life.
Their husky voices and weathered faces
replace grandfathers I never knew.

They laugh loud, curse, talk about
their single life, but I can see that
they love the way the light fades in the canyon
and how the candles mother always places on the table
light our faces, and how lucky they think my father is.

The men who never marry,
who live in studio apartments in Hollywood
with no responsibilities,
find it difficult to leave when the dishes are cleared
and we begin to yawn.

Sometimes they stay for Ed Sullivan,
but more often they stand and stretch,
their still-firm stomachs show as they lift their arms
then squat down to say

"Good night kid, sleep tight,
see you at the beach next weekend."

Humphrey jumped down from the wall and meowed at the plate glass door. It was too heavy for me to open, so Mommy stopped our practice to let him in. With the door open we heard a car.

"It's daddy!" I cried. I ran to the front office and looked out to see the yellow and white Chevy crossing our bridge. Before he could pull into the garage I was back in the studio, adjusting my daisies.

Mommy waited until she heard the front door open, then she dropped the needle on the record and quickly got back into place.

And then there he was, my tall, handsome father, in his white shorts, and white zories, and brown and white Hawaiian shirt. His curly brown hair was wet from showering at the gym.

As Peggy Lee crooned, Daddy smiled. Automatically, without being asked, he walked over to his camera stand and rolled it into the middle of the room. He sat behind it on a stool, with his long legs outstretched. He bent over the Hasselblad which made a loud click every time he took a picture.

My daisies stayed put and I remembered most of the steps. An excited Humphrey ran in and out of the frame. On the contact sheet you can see him, with his tail high in the air, trying to catch mother's scarf.

When the song ended, Daddy lifted his face and saw us in person, right side up. He smiled and clapped. Mommy went over and gave him a kiss. Ann, feeling shy, put her arm briefly around him, then went to change her clothes. I waited until she was gone then hugged him around the waist.

"Can we see the pictures tonight?" I asked. The only thing I liked almost as much as having my picture taken was getting to watch Daddy make prints in the dark room.

He said, "Sid Cesar is on tonight. I'll develop the film after dinner, then make the prints tomorrow."

In bed, with Humphrey curled up by my feet, it took a while to fall asleep. I kept wondering how the pictures would turn out. I could hear Mommy and Daddy laughing at the TV. I wished the show would end so he would go into the darkroom and develop the film!

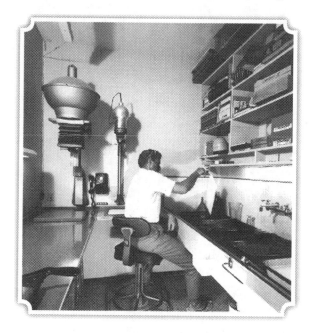

In complete pitch-dark he could open the camera, extract the roll and only by feel, wind it onto the metal spool. Then he'd slide the spool into a long, cold stainless-steel cylinder. The sound of metal on metal made a terrible screech. He'd pour foul smelling developer into the can and never spill a drop. Then he'd rock the cylinder back and forth—clang, clang, clang—making sure every bit of film got wet.

Only after the film had been in the cylinder for a specified time, and he had flushed it with cold water, could the door be opened. Then Daddy would pull out the spools and unwind the film. Two-and-a-quarter film had only twelve shots, so it wasn't very long; but 35mm could have up to thirty-six frames, so it was very long and skinny. Each strip was hung from a wooden clothes pin permanently fastened above the sink. Once dry, Daddy would cut the film into shorter strips and slide them into cloudy envelopes. A special fine-tipped black-ink pen was used to label the envelopes.

I finally fell asleep, happy to imagine Daddy in his pitch black cavern, performing his magic.

In the morning I found Daddy in the kitchen, cutting oranges. Mommy was scrambling eggs.

"When are we going to print our pictures?" I asked.

"Let him eat breakfast!" Ann said coming into the kitchen in her baby doll pajamas. I poured myself a bowl of Wheat Chex and found fresh blueberries in the refrigerator.

"I'll run the color shots over to the lab," Mommy told Daddy.

"Can you drop me off in Westwood?" Ann asked.

"If you're ready in twenty minutes," Mommy told her. Ann began to whine and pretty soon they were arguing, so I took my bowl outside and sat cross legged on the cement by the pool. Humphrey came and sat beside me. I let him lick my empty bowl. When I came back in the house Mommy said, "Peter's printing the pictures from last night."

I plopped my bowl in the sink and ran to the dark rooms. I watched Daddy unscrew black plastic lids from huge brown jugs and splash pungent chemicals into waiting trays. He lifted me up so I could sit on the counter, while he moved like a wizard in the long skinny room.

He flipped on an amber light and slid the door closed. He pushed a towel into the little gap at the bottom of the door, and sat his tall frame on a heavy metal stool to begin his craft.

First he made a contact sheet so we could see all the pictures. He laid the negative strips in a glass frame, put a sheet of paper over them, pressed down the top, secured it and flipped the whole thing over. For a few seconds the room was filled with light. Then he took the back off of the frame and slipped the sheet of paper into the developer. I craned my neck to see, as he used plastic tongs to gently move the paper around.

"P.U!" I said because of the nasty smell.

"Developer, then hypo, then fix," he told me, using his tongs to transfer the paper from tray to tray. Daddy peered at the wet sheet for a while and said, "Let's enlarge number six."

This time he took one of the negative strips and put it in a holder, then slide it into the enlarger. First he did a test on regular paper—big black bellows descended and contracted as he turned a dial, focusing. We looked so creepy! The white wall of the studio looked black, our teeth looked black, the black ribbon around my chest was white. Everything was reversed.

Once it was in focus, he turned off the enlarger light and we were plunged into the eerie amber glow again. Then he placed the special heavy paper in the frame and positioned it under the enlarger. He turned the dial on a wall-mounted timer that sounded like a hissing snake, and cool white light was released into the chilly room. My cold bare feet, with pink painted toenails, dangled far above the linoleum.

I wanted to crawl into my father's lap like I did sometimes after dinner, and nuzzle into him but I knew I couldn't because he was working. Then he stood and slid the paper into the first sick smelling bath.

I wanted to see the picture! But I had to wait. It took time. Then, finally, he placed the sheet into the last tray, where clean, clear water ran and the paper bobbed like a person drowning. With tongs, Daddy turned it over and lifted the print for me to see and there we were: mommy, and Ann, and I. We *did* look like the June Taylor Dancers!

In a little room between the two darkrooms sat a huge drum dryer. Daddy lifted me up onto the work counter with its built-in light box for viewing color transparencies. I watched as he turned a dial near the wall, then struck a wooden match and stuck it into an opening in the shiny drum—*poof!* and then blue flames. He let me blow out the match. Then he reached up and opened the high transom louvers, and cool ocean air blew in. When the drum was hot enough, Daddy pulled a cord to start the canvas rolling. Back in the darkroom, he lifted prints out of the rinse water and pressed them against the fiberglass wall of the sink. He used his flat hand to push off excess water. This he called "squeegee-ing". He brought the prints out to the dryer, and carefully placed each one, face down, patting out air bubbles, making them completely flat. We watched as they disappeared, eaten up by the fiery monster.

"If it's too wet, it will stick." I told him. "And you can burn your fingers trying to get it off!"

"That's right," he replied.

But this time the prints came out perfectly. One by one they fell into the square wire basket, like petals falling off a flower. I was allowed to place them on the counter to cool.

When I look at those pictures now, I can almost hear Peggy Lee crooning and my sister's high heels clicking on the terrazzo. I can see my mother's pink scarf and smell her Breck shampoo, as she kneels before me, pinning daisies on a ribbon, so we can do a dance for Daddy.

Chapter 5

GLAMOR GIRL

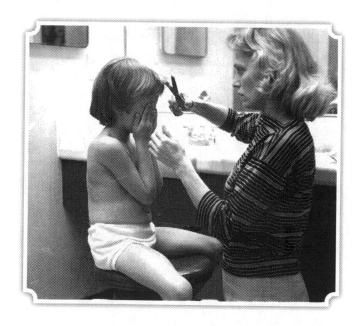

As a newborn, dark brown hair covered my head. By the age of two it had become blond and wavy. Once a week, Mother took me into the shower with her, to shampoo my hair. Then we'd go through the painful ritual of combing out the tangles. I'd cry and push her away. We tried using old fashioned remedies, rinsing with vinegar or beer, but nothing helped. Not until 1960 did *Life*, an anti-tangle crème rinse in a blue plastic bottle, come onto the market.

By age six, Mother finally got tired of struggling with my tangles and decided to cut my hair short. I sat on a piano stool in the models' dressing room and put my fingers over my eyes. The sound of the her good sewing scissors made me cringe with each snip.

I hated my haircut. I missed my tresses. Mother told me it was very chic and European. But I thought I looked awful. To make matters worse, my teeth started to fall out.

The rusty, salty taste horrified me. Yet I also found it kind of interesting. I knew all my baby teeth would eventually be replaced by permanent adult ones that were hidden somewhere up in my skull. When I pressed my tongue against a loose tooth the nauseating wiggle told me an awkward, ugly phase of my life was starting. What if I never outgrew it?

One day my parents and I went to one of our favorite restaurants, Ted's Grill, a block from State Beach. They served thick New England clam chowder and steak sandwiches on chewy sourdough bread. For dessert there were always trays of hot, fresh cobbler—cherry, blueberry, and apple.

Cool, dim Ted's Grill had a bar attached. If my parents wanted to have a drink before dinner, I happily entertained myself gazing into the three-D viewer inside the front door. It had dozens of black and white photos of the olden days. I liked recognizing buildings that still stood, and imagining what it must have been like to live way back then, before jetties and the pier, when Pacific Coast Highway was just two lanes and trolley tracks connected the city to the beach.

On this particular day my parents decided to eat at the counter instead of at our usual red booth by the windows. As my father lifted me onto the round leather stool, I slipped and my face came down hard on the counter. I cried out, and put my hand to my mouth. Blood! Mother staunched it with a napkin and a kindly waitress wrapped ice in a towel and handed it to her. Tears streamed down my face as the ice numbed me.

Mother led me out through the patio to the ladies' room which was more like the restroom at State Beach. It had a gritty cement floor and hammered-tin over the sink instead of a real mirror. Mother patted my face and took a look at me. My lower teeth had cut the inside of my upper lip. The bleeding had stopped but the lip had started to swell.

She consoled me, gave me a hug, and we went back into the restaurant. I didn't like being hurt but I did like the attention. My father offered to spoon-feed me clam chowder until I told him I was okay and could feed myself.

After lunch we walked over to my parents' best friends' apartment. We went up the long staircase to the tiny landing. On the left side was a plain apartment door. On the right Jo had covered the door with turquoise and white Hawaiian fabric. We jingled the string of Indian brass bells and opened the door. I don't remember it ever being locked.

Jo Lathwood had suntan skin and short blond hair. She made her own colorful cotton clothes. She looked up from her sewing machine. Tall, slouchy Benjie stopped typing at his little desk.

"You look like a boxer who just lost a match!" Benjie said.

Jo went to the closet and brought out one of Bengie's tweed jackets and put it on me. Daddy took pictures of me hamming it up. I liked making them laugh. If I couldn't be pretty, at least I could funny.

By the time I was eight, my hair had grown long again. I wanted it to look like Darlene on the Mickey Mouse Club. Her long hair was "V" shaped, longer in the back. I didn't want to ask my mother to cut it, because I knew she'd hack it short again, so I asked my fifteen-year-old sister, Ann to cut it.

I didn't mention Darlene. I said, "Ann, could you cut my hair like yours?" for hers looked like Darlene's—long and curled under with bangs. Ann was always pretty and fashionable. She wore a long, straight, wool skirt, and a pastel pink sweater, bobby socks and saddle shoes. Around her neck she wore a cute darker pink scarf.

I could not see myself in the mirror as she started to snip. I kept my gaze down and saw clumps of hair fall around me.

"I think you're cutting too much," I said.

"Stop moving," she commanded.

"I'm not," I cried, for I was trying to be still as a statue.

"There!" Ann said and gave me a hand mirror. An icy chill ran through me. She had cut my hair like Buster Brown again!

"I wanted to look like Darlene and now I look like a boy again. I hate you!"

I ran into my room and threw myself on the bed. Why had I let her touch my hair? Now I'd never be pretty. I'd probably never have a boyfriend or get married or be happy. I was doomed to be alone.

Humphrey, who had been sleeping on the bed, jumped onto the floor and stretched. I laid down beside him. I put my face on his chest and listened to his soothing, rhythmic purr.

EIGHT

When I am eight
I pretend I'm married.
I put my cat
under the covers.
His fur is the back
of my husband's head,
his purr is snoring,
his body hot.

Sometime in the night
the cat escapes.
My nightgown rides up.
I am bare, hairless.
I sleep alone
on the other side
of my parents' wall
where my mother
clings
to my father's back.

Before I go to sleep
I put my new shoes
next to my bed
so they are the first things I see
when I open my eyes.

My shoes are waiting
for my feet, just as
I am waiting for my legs
to stop aching
for my breasts
to start growing
so men will look at me
because
I know what men want.

Someday I will be married.
I will have a man
who will stick himself in me.

I hope it doesn't hurt
because I am tired of hurting.

I am tired of being a child.

I turned on my little TV. I plugged in the square, green, corduroy pillow with a speaker in it. My father had photographed it for *Mechanics Illustrated*. We got to keep the items that were featured in the "Mimi" column. Every month, the same pretty girl, dressed in striped overalls with nothing underneath, and a conductor's hat, held some new gadget that was reviewed.

I turned the dial to Channel 7, and caught the beginning of *Glamour Girl*, a daily show, on which three women told their sad stories, in hopes they would win a makeover. Based on their stories, the audience decided which one would get to come back the next day, and be transformed.

At the end of the show the host announced that there would be a special episode for girls. My ears perked up. I grabbed a pencil and wrote down where to send my letter. I turned off the TV and started writing . . .

The day the mail came telling me that I had been chosen as a contestant, I couldn't believe it. I was so happy.

The day we went to the set Mother made sure I looked as plain as possible. She dressed me in a drab cardigan, buttoned all the way up, and put a bobby pin on each side of my bangs. The outfit and my glasses made me look studious, definitely not glamorous.

We drove to Burbank. Mother gave our name to the guard at the gate. We entered the big production lot with its huge warehouses and sound stages. Actors and technicians used golf carts to drive from place to place. Men rolled clothing racks from one set to another. Extras in costumes crisscrossed in front of us, as we looked for the right parking lot.

A representative of the show greeted us—a pretty young woman in high heels and a circle-skirt that swept her calves. She asked if I was nervous—kind of. Mother could wait in the "Green Room," and watch the live program on close-circuit TV.

The set was simple: a blue-green curtain as backdrop with a sign in script that said *Glamour Girl*, and two chairs at center stage. The director told me and the other two contestants to sit on the three chairs at stage right.

"That red light over the lens means the camera is on," he said. I had never seen such gigantic cameras in my life. There were two of them on heavy-duty roll-around stands and thick black cables all over the floor.

As always, the show began with a "reveal." On stage left an easel held a black and white blow up of yesterday's contestant. Her expression was grim. The host gave a brief recap and then the curtain parted. The audience burst into applause. The dowdy woman now looked like Eva Gardner, with bright red lipstick, short wavy hair, a rhinestone necklace and a shimmering off-the-shoulder gown. I wanted to look like *that*. The announcer rattled off the list of her other prizes and then her family rushed onto the stage for much hugging and kissing. She waved to the audience and blew a kiss, then the happy group departed back through the curtain.

The host called the first girl, a pretty Asian nine-year-old with long shiny hair. She took her seat next to him. He used a hand-held mike as he interviewed her. She spoke in a sweet, soft voice about her family having to move out of state, because of her father's new job.

If she won the make-over, she'd give herself a going-away party. The second contestant's dark hair contrasted with her pasty skin. She spoke with shoulders slumped in a barely audible voice. Also nine, she had recently recovered from leukemia and wanted to celebrate with a new hairdo and wardrobe. Both the girls came from out of state. They each received polite applause.

I could not see the audience because of the bright, hot lights. But they didn't bother me. I was used to lights and performing in front of people, if only at my parents' parties. I took my seat by the announcer.

"Mary Lee Gowland," the host began, "Why do you want to be a Glamour Girl?"

I explained as I had rehearsed, "My father is a famous photographer. He photographs beautiful women. I want to be beautiful, too, but my sister cut off my hair!"

The audience let out a collective, sympathetic moan.

"And, are you a native?" the host asked.

"Of course not!" I replied. "Natives live in Africa."

The audience burst out laughing. I hadn't meant to be funny but the sound of their laughter in that big hollow sound stage felt good.

After each of us had given our testimony, we returned to our seats and the hostess wheeled out an applause meter. The announcer stood behind each of our chairs and the meter registered the sound of the audience clapping.

I won! The show ended with me smiling into the hot white lights as the theme song kicked in. Mother appeared and I followed her into an office where the first woman who greeted us explained what would happen the next day. I could hardly sleep that night wondering how my transformation would turn out.

In the morning Mother drove me back to the TV studios and handed me over to a pretty blonde woman. I don't remember her name, so I'll call her Marie. Marie told Mother she didn't need to stay, as it would take at least three hours to undergo my transformation. Mother gave me a hug and said she'd be back with Daddy and Ann before the show started.

First, Marie took me to have my eyes examined, so I could get prettier glasses. I wanted cat's-eye glasses like I'd seen Marilyn Monroe wear. The eye doctor was tall with red cheeks. He removed my glasses and asked me to read a chart on the wall. Then he lowered the big metal device and pressed it close to my face. To this day I experience anxiety when I'm asked "Which is better, this way, or this way?" afraid that I'll say the wrong thing and my prescription will be all wrong.

When the doctor pulled the big machine away from my eyes he said, "I don't think you'll need glasses until you're forty. Just sit near the front of the class and you'll be able to see the blackboard." He was off by a few years. I got my first distance prescription at twenty-six, but at the time I was delighted.

Next, Marie took me to a fitting room where I met a bald man with a German accent and a tape measure hanging around his neck. I stood on a box with my arms out while he measured me, just like my mother did when she made me dresses.

By now it was lunchtime. Marie took me into the commissary, a big cafeteria. The room was filled with actors and actresses, many in costume. I hoped I'd see Leo G. Carroll, who played *Topper*, or Phyllis Kirk who played Nora Charles on *The Thin Man*, or Jayne Meadows from *The Honeymooners,* even though I forgot to bring my autograph book. So far I had autographs of Tab Hunter and Rock Hudson, two handsome actors who'd come to our house to be photographed.

Marie took me through the cafeteria line and said I could eat anything I wanted. I hardly had an appetite but I chose fish sticks, corn and lemon meringue pie. Mostly I just drank milk to calm the butterflies in my stomach.

After lunch Marie took me to the beauty salon, located in a big trailer. The hairdresser was a young woman with bright red hair. The mirror in front of my big leather barber chair had been covered with a black cloth. They wanted me to be surprised.

The hairdresser rolled my hair onto pink plastic rollers and doused it with permanent wave solution that smelled like eggs. While it was setting, she lit a cigarette and sat in a chair next to me while I peppered her with questions about the famous people she knew.

In order to reach the rinse sink I sat on a red bolster that had been used by Lauren Chapin, from *Father Knows Best*, and other young actresses. Then the hairdresser trimmed my hair and styled it.

"You look great kid!" she said, as she sent me to the makeup trailer next door. The makeup man was thin with soft hands. He spoke in a soothing voice, telling me that first, I would get a facial. I knew about facials. Sometimes, on Sundays when it was too cold to go to the beach, Mother gave me and my friends facials. She'd whip up egg yolks and spread them on our faces. They dried into a hard yellow mask. We had to try not to laugh and crack the mask before it worked its wonders. Then, we rinsed our faces in cool water. Our skin felt soft and smooth as a baby's.

This time, though, what the makeup man spread on my face smelled like roses. I leaned my head back and closed my eyes as his gentle hands spread the pink cream all over my face. As it dried he massaged my hands and trimmed my fingernails. He wiped off the facial crème and used a cotton ball to apply witch hazel that smelled fresh and made my skin tingle. Then he applied light foundation and pale pink lipstick. I wanted to see what I looked like!

Marie came into the trailer holding a garment bag. She hung it on a peg and unzipped it. Then she took out the most beautiful dress I had ever seen—pale blue dotted Swiss with a square neck decorated with roses, a fitted bodice, puffy sleeves, and a full skirt. It took my breath away.

I went behind a folding screen to change. There, on a chair, was a new pair of white lace underpants, a white slip and white lace-trimmed socks. I put my pleated skirt and white blouse in a bag, along with my socks and saddle shoes. When I slipped into the new clothes I felt like a princess.

I came out from behind the screen to *oohs* and *ahhs* from Marie and the makeup man. Marie handed me a pair of black patent leather Mary Janes. She even knelt down and buckled them for me.

Together we walked to the sound stage where *Glamour Girl* was already underway. Backstage I could hear the announcer. Then, it was time: the curtain parted and there I stood in all my glory. The audience applauded. I smiled, held out the edges of my skirt and turned slowly so everyone could see the big bow in the back.

As my parents and sister came on stage I saw myself in a big gilt mirror. The roses on my dress matched my pale pink lipstick. Perfect.

Ann looked embarrassed when the announcer said, "So, you're the big sister who cut her hair!"

The announcer held an eleven-by-fourteen black and white of me from the day before and held it next to me so the audience could see the amazing transformation.

He listed the rest of my prizes, displayed in a pyramid. My favorite was the pink rain coat with *Singing in the Rain* written in rhinestones along the hem. Finally, we all waved to the audience and departed back stage.

I wore my beautiful princess dress for our third and fourth grade class pictures and reluctantly surrendered it to Good Will when it no longer fit. By then full skirts were out of style and we all wanted to look like Jackie Kennedy in her sleek, elegant Chanel and Christian Dior designs.

Chapter 6

EUROPE ON FIVE DOLLARS A DAY

On January 1, 1959, I start marking down the days before the trip on a little blackboard in my bedroom, my cat Humphrey watching with his yellow eyes. I become more and more sick to my stomach as our departure date approaches. I am nine.

"I don't want to go!" I say to my mother one night, when she's cooking dinner.

"Don't start, Mary Lee," she says, turning away from the stove in our galley style kitchen. "Everything is set. We're going to have a wonderful time." She points to the earmarked copy of *Europe on Five Dollars a Day* on the counter. "Look at all the places we're going to visit! The Louvre, The Leaning Tower of Pisa, The Coliseum, Tivoli Gardens . . ."

"I don't care about Tivoli Gardens." I yell. "You can send postcards."

"You're being ridiculous. We're not leaving you behind." Just then we hear my sixteen-year-old sister Ann drive up in her little white MG.

She comes in the house, carrying her school books.

"It'll be cheaper if you leave me home" I say, trying a new tact. "Ann can stay with me. She doesn't want to go either. She doesn't want to leave Dell or the drill team."

"I'm not staying here with you." Ann says dismissively. "I want to see Europe and meet our English relatives. You're being a brat." She goes into her room and closes the door.

"I want to stay here." I yell. "Why can't Andy come and stay with me?"

"Oh honestly," my mother says. "You're giving me a headache."

"I hate you!" I cry and run into my room. Humphrey is sleeping on the bed but wakes up when I slam the door. I lie down on the bed next to him. My loyal cat.

Ever since finding out about the trip I've had swollen glands and been sick to my stomach. Mother took me to the Ross Loos Medical Group, a pale pink stucco building on Wilshire Boulevard. I watched as vials of my blood were drawn. They couldn't find anything wrong. The black haired doctor prescribed a molasses based elixir and extra-rich milk.

I tell Humphrey, "I'm going to get Andy to come and stay with us." He closes his eyes, rolls over and shows me his stomach. I stroke his belly. The first time I saw him, it was raining. We heard a tiny sound. My father opened the front door and a little black kitten ran in the house and hid under the couch. I got down on the floor and peered at those two bright, round yellow eyes. I was only three but I remember thinking, _this is not a doll, this is real!_

"We can have someone drive us to the market." I tell Humphrey, because I know my grandmother doesn't drive. Andy is my father's mother. She was born in England. When she came to American she changed her name to Sylvia Andrew, so we call her Andy. She lives in a silver trailer in Santa Monica. I love to visit and sit across from

44

her at the tiny table under the sloping roof. When she serves tea she pours the milk into the cup first, then the dark brown tea that smells so good. She has deep set pale turquoise eyes and a kind smile. Her fingers are wrinkly and crooked but gentle when she combs my hair. I was really sad when she was locked up in the asylum in Camarillo. I remember waiting outside on the green rolling lawn while my parents visited, looking up at the barred windows, hoping to see her face. My parents were very relieved when the shock treatments worked and she didn't hose down people in the street anymore, or think her phone was tapped.

Thinking about Andy coming to stay with me calms me down. I go back into the kitchen and don't even have to be asked to set the table. When I use the electric can opener Humphrey bolts into the kitchen. He follows me as I carry the food outside. His wife, a wild cat I call Twitchy, comes running down from the canyon. I squat down and she comes over to me. I'm the only one who can touch her. I stroke her stripped fur. Her tail flips back and forth. If I forget to feed her, she'll leap onto the screen door and hang there. We're used to it and think it's funny, but it scares guests or people who don't know her. As she and Humphrey start to eat, two of their kittens come out from under the big Elephant Ear plant and join them.

When I come back in the house my mother says, "Mary Lee, go tell Peter dinner's ready." So I go out the front door, down the steps and into the garage where my father is perched on a tall stool at his workbench.

"Dinner's ready." I tell him. He's wearing what he always wears, white zories even though it's February. He hates shoes. He looks up from the camera he's working on and says, "Ok. I'll be there in a minute."

During dinner my mother and father go over more details of the trip:

We'll fly from Los Angeles to Kansas City where Daddy will lecture to a camera club. Then take another plane to Buffalo, New York. Then fly to New York City and stay a week. Then we are taking a "jet" to Germany, where our brand new car will be waiting.

45

"I've talked to your teacher," mother says to me. "She thinks this is a wonderful idea and you'll learn a lot. She's getting your lessons ready so Ann and I can tutor you."

I stare down into my spaghetti, afraid if I look at her I'll start arguing again. I don't mind leaving school. Fourth grade is boring. I've been staying home a lot lately, with an upset stomach or swollen glands. It's much more interesting at home. From the kitchen I can look through our long, low house and see Daddy taking pictures in the studio. This year Tab Hunter and Rock Hudson came to the house. I got both their autographs. I like to listen to Mother in the office, talking to clients and models on the phone. I love to watch their assistant, Dale, making prints in the darkroom, or Lane helping build cameras in the garage. And when Bea comes once a week, she lets me help her iron.

If I go on the trip, which I don't plan to, I *will* miss my next door neighbors, Sue and Teresa, who go to the Catholic school. On weekends we have a lot of fun dressing up and taking pictures. Last summer Mother took pictures of us dressed up like movie stars. Because I'm blonde, I was Marilyn Monroe, and made a perfect pouty mouth. Sue and Teresa, brunettes, were Sophia Loren and Gina Lollabrigida. Mommy piled their hair up, messy, and posed them down in the creek, in long skirts and white blouses pulled off their shoulders. She's going to write an article and send the pictures to Life Magazine.

So, even though I'll miss my friends, *if I go,* I can write to them and we'll be back in time for summer.

My *cats* are the problem. You can't write letters to cats. Just thinking about leaving them makes my stomach hard as a rock. Supposedly the man and woman who will stay in our house will take care of them. But no one can take care of them or love them like I do.

After dinner, before "Dobie Gillis", I sneak into my parents' bedroom and call Andy. She says "Hello?" almost in a whisper.

"Hi Andy, it's me," I say quickly. "I have a plan . . ."

I start to tell her my idea of her staying with me, but she interrupts. "Darling, Bubba," she says using my nickname. "Your mummy and daddy would never think of leaving you behind! They would miss you too much. They love you and want to take you on an adventure!" I start to interrupt but she'll have none of it, deepening her voice, "Now, my sweet, don't act like a little scardey-cat! Don't you want to see the house where I grew up and meet my brothers and your cousins?"

"No!" I say emphatically. "I want to stay home, with you."

"Mary Lee" she says sternly, "You're almost ten years old. Be brave. And write me letters. I'll write you back, I promise."

My heart sinks. The one person who I thought would surely understand has sided with *them*.

The weekend before we leave, my parents' best friends Jo and Benjie come to dinner. They're back from their annual winter in a tropical place, where Jo paints and Benjie writes and catches their dinner with his spear fishing gun. Benjie jokes around with me. He smells like rum and coke and cigarettes. "Bubb," he says, and holds out his fist. I look down at his suntanned hand. When he opens his fingers there's a little brown and white shell. "From Tahiti" he says. I take it and look into his eyes. "What will you bring *me* from Europe?"

Two days before we leave, in spite of a fever from the last typhus/typhoid shot, I'm whisked off to do a TV commercial for a toy called "Froggy". I get to wear the dotted Swiss dress I won on "Glamour Girl" the year before. I stand beside Don Fell smiling down into an aquarium, as he squeezes a green rubber ball that pumps into the little frog man. For this I earn $25.00!

We depart on Wednesday, taking three cars to the airport. Mommy and I ride with Sue and Teresa's parents, Pat and Charlie, baby Monty on Pat's lap. Ann rides with her boyfriend Dell, who's the star quarterback of the Uni High football team. Daddy rides with Dale. Jo and Benjie bring Andy. It's always a big production when someone goes to the airport. Last year when Jo and Benjie came back from Hawaii, Mommy dressed us up in 1920's costumes, "We're missionaries!" she said.

At the airport, I hug Andy. She hands me a present, a flat package I tuck under my arm. We cross the tarmac and climb the stairs to the plane. Mother stops just as we're about to go in, "Wave!" she says, taking my shoulders and turning me toward the crowd gathered behind the chain link fence. Everyone's smiling and waving. Everyone except Andy, who's crying. She puts a handkerchief to her nose. I feel sad and mad at the same time, but I blow her a kiss and, feeling Benjie's shell in my pocket, go into the plane. I sit looking out the window as the propellers start to turn. They make an incredible noise as we lift off. Then everything on earth looks like a doll-sized town as we ascend into the sky. I unwrap the present from Andy, a small pink hot water bottle with the Three Little Pigs embossed on it.

The first two weeks I have a lot to write home about: a tornado in Kansas City and a blizzard in Buffalo, where Daddy is on two TV shows. In New York Mommy, Ann and I go shopping and I get a pinch-waist navy blue coat with a matching hat that ties under my chin. I love the music and dancing in "West Side Story" on Broadway, even though the end makes me cry. We take our first ride on a subway and walk over steam coming up through the sidewalks. It's exciting to go up to the top of the Empire State Building where the wind whips our hair around. F.A.O Schwartz is a big toy store but very expensive. "We can buy these exact toys in Germany" Mommy says when I eye some Steiff stuffed animals.

In a big auditorium, just before Mommy and Daddy are supposed to give a photography lecture, they ask Ann to put on her two-piece bathing suit and stand in for the model who Mommy says "looks like a hooker." Ann rolls her eyes, but is a good sport. She has pretty white teeth and knows how to pose. I watch from back stage and feel proud of my family. Afterwards there's a special banquet in our honor with an amazing dessert: ice cream covered with meringue and browned in the oven, called Baked Alaska because Alaska has just become a state.

The real trip begins when we take a jet to Paris and a prop plane to Frankfurt, then a train to Stuttgart. It's exciting to feel the rattle of the wheels beneath us and look out the window at cows and old fashioned houses. After we check into our hotel, Daddy leaves. He comes back in a little while with our brand new blue Mercedes 190 four-door car. Before we get in it, Daddy has us pose beside it, to show what fits: tall, handsome Daddy, wearing a suit and tie and a bowler hat, then Mommy and Ann, with their New York haircuts, in straight wool skirts, stockings and flats, holding big satchel-purses. Then me in elastic-waist pants and a dark blue cardigan sweater. In front of us, five suit cases, three camera cases and two portable typewriters. Daddy puts the Hasselblad on the tripod, hits the shutter delay and then gets in the picture.

The weather is cold. It starts to rain. I sit in the back seat on the right side, staring out the window, wondering how my cats are. Wondering if Andy has gotten my letters. I put Benjie's shell in the door ash tray so I won't lose it. Ann sits on the left side, staring out her window and writing letters to Dell. The car smells of new leather and Ann's Jean Naté cologne.

At the hotel Ann and I have to share a bed so we put pillows between us. The cover of the bed is puffy, full of feathers. I sleep with my Three Little Pigs hot water bottle clutched to my stomach, because it's starting to hurt again. At breakfast, the family eats at a round table with a white lace table cloth. We order hot chocolate, but it's so thick, almost like pudding so Mommy orders hot milk and we mix them together.

Ann is anxious to get to Munich where she hopes to get a letter from Dell and of course I want to get one from Andy. We'll celebrate Daddy's forty-third birthday there. We lug our suitcases up the stairs to our adjoining rooms, and leave the door open between them. We've only been there a few minutes when there's a knock on the door: a telegram from America!

All of us stop what we're doing as Daddy says *"Danke schöen"* and gives the man a five Mark coin. I sit on Mommy and Daddy's bed. My heart starts beating fast. Daddy hands the telegram to Mommy and sits on the bed beside me.

Mommy reads the telegram and then looks up. Her mouth falls open.

"Andy died." she says. I can't hear the rest of what she says because my head is pounding so loud, it feels like my head will explode. Mommy has her arms around Daddy and Ann is leading me into our room. She closes the door behind us.

Then she does something she never does. She hugs me. I stand stunned in the arms of my sixteen year old sister trying to hear what she's saying but the blood in my head is so loud that I have to throw up. I push away from her and run into the bathroom where I lift the black toilet seat and feel a disgusting hot rush come up my throat. I turn on the cold water faucet and rinse my mouth. When I turn it off I hear Ann crying.

Mommy comes into our room. Her eyes are red. I run to her and put my arms around her waist. She speaks slowly.

"Andy got sick. Jo and Benjie took her to the hospital. But it was too late. She had an intestinal blockage." She blows her nose.

"When?" Ann asks.

"Two days ago. She'll be buried tomorrow. They bought her a dress."

She blows her nose again. "Dark blue with white polka dots."

I push away from her and open the door to their room. My father is sitting on the bed, his head in his hands, crying. I've never seen my father cry before. But instead of wanting to go to him, I'm suddenly furious. What I'm thinking is, *you killed her! She didn't want us to go away! She was crying when we left. Going away is what made her sick. If we had been home she wouldn't have died. You killed her. I hate you!*

Mommy walks past me to go sit on the bed next to Daddy. I close the door.

Later, at dinner, which is hideous looking sausages and smelly cabbage, Mommy tells us that there's no point in going home. There's nothing we can do. Jo and Benjie are taking care of everything. By "everything" I know she means packing up her trailer. Please God, I think, don't let them throw her poems away!

Within a week, I'm sick. Food passes right through me. I start a collection of toilet paper. Some is as rough as gas station paper towels. Some is slick as wax paper. Some is translucent and frail as tissue paper. A big fat German doctor comes to the hotel. His prescription: I must eat grated apples. As we drive to our next destination, I sit on my side of the car, grating apples with a white grater into a blue plastic bowl until they turn brown and mushy. I can barely choke them down. I begin to hate the smell of apples.

My parents try giving me *Liebfraumilch,* the sweet German wine, before dinner, to see if it will stimulate my appetite. But the smell of the heavy food makes me nauseas. My mother learns this phrase—and I do too because she has to say it at every new hotel: *"Mein tocktor est kronk und darf ner ein diet laben. Volen zie bitte, cooken das a hafferflacken, ein minuten, oner gewirtz."* Which means, "My daughter is sick and on a strict diet. Will you please cook this oatmeal one minute, without spice?" So! Gewirtz is the word for spice. I have a friend at school named *Kathie* Gewirtz! She's new, from back East and wears long brown braids and brown shoes.

I'm sick through Furstenfelbruk, Füssen, Zurich, The Italian Swiss Colony, Venice, Florence and Rome. It rains a lot. In Venice we see glass blowers and some teenagers flirt with Ann.

In Rome the Coliseum is dank and cold. At the hotel there is a German Shepherd and a white kitten. This is the first cat I've seen in 36 days. I hold the kitten to my chest and feel its purr. This makes me feel both better and worse because I want *my own cats!*

I hope they're ok. I've written to Sue and Teresa asking them to go over and check on them, but I've not heard back. I miss my home and my grandmother's dead. I will never again have tea with her in her shiny silver trailer.

One day, I open my suitcase and find that I've lost my Three Pigs hot water bottle. All I have now is Benjie's shell, rattling around in the ashtray as we drive through Livorno and Portofino and arrive in Santa Margherita Ligure on the Golfo de Genoa.

On the third day of eating *nothing*, I begin to believe that if I speak, if I empty myself of the words inside me, I will deflate, the membrane of my skin will collapse and I will be like a scarf, forgotten on the floor. So I am silent. Outside the white hotel there are many small fishing boats and sea gulls. I sip water. I draw. I sit on the cold toilet and look at my pale, blue feet dangling above white tiles shaped like honeycomb. Finally, an American doctor is called. She has silver hair and kind eyes. She reminds me of Andy. I love her immediately. She sits next to me on the bed and holds my hand.

"How are you feeling Mary Lee?" she asks. I look at her and start to cry.

"I want to go home." I tell her. She hands me a white handkerchief.

"This child must go to the hospital." she tells my parents.

"But we have an itinerary." Mommy says. The doctor and my parents leave the room. In a few minutes the American doctor comes back alone. "I'm going to give you a treatment", she says, "that will make you better."

Later, when I write about this is my diary, I'm so embarrassed I cross out the word. I must lie on my side and let her put water in me. As she does this she asks, "Do you like Annette?" and I know she's talking about the Mousketeers.

"I like Cubby and Karen," I answer. I don't understand how this will cure me, but I'm so weak and tired, I lie there on the soft Italian bed, and look at the mirror on the wall, reflecting sun shimmering on the Ligurian Sea.

Later, my parents and sister return and plop down their coats and cameras. They're cheerful. They tell me about the town. "There's going to be a bonfire tonight!" I watch from the hotel window. The whole town is singing and carrying on. Embers fly up and die in the ink black sky.

The next day when the American doctor comes she has a smile on her face. A few minutes later there's a knock on the door. A small man in a red jacket wheels in a cart. He smiles at me and says something in Italian. The doctor fluffs my pillows. Then she takes the silver cover off a dinner plate and the room is filled with the most delicious smell: roast chicken. My mouth begins to water. My stomach rumbles. The doctor places a tray over my lap and sets down a thick white plate. On it is a breast of chicken, a fluffy mound of mashed potatoes with a pat of butter melting, and a pot of tea. At first it seems enough to just look at the food. The colors are so vivid. The doctor and my parents watch as I pick up the heavy silver fork. I taste the food. I look up at my parents. I smile. Everyone sighs. I am suddenly part of the world again. We will spend my tenth birthday in Paris, after all.

The improvement in my health is immediate. In the morning I wake up hungry and will have an appetite all the way through France. We drive through Monaco and see Princess Grace's yacht. We walk on the rocky beach in Nice. We're given a tour of the Bolex Camera and Typewriter factory and taken out to dinner afterwards. My sister and I are given music boxes.

We arrive in Paris on April 28th and check into a beautiful room with a balcony. At the Follies Brigere, we see *Cyrano de Bergerac* ballet, at the Louvre, the *Mona Lisa* and *Venus de Milo*. There's a long line at the Eiffel Tower so we don't go up. On my tenth birthday I pick out a nylon nightie and a French doll. I'm thrilled that we get a twenty-percent discount because we pay with Traveler's Checks.

In Notre Dame Cathedral we run into our neighbors, the Warrens. Harve is a set designer. His wife, Marge, is a housewife. Mommy says, "It's incredible how Marge spends her days clipping coupons and drives all over town just to save ten cents." We're so amazed to run into them!

The next day, driving to see the sights, Mommy composes this limerick on the Olivetti Underwood on her lap:

> *There once was a woman named Marge*
> *Who was built like the back of a barge*
> *She had as much taste as bowlful of paste*
> *And Harve always called her "The Sarge"*

Our lunch, at an outdoor café, feels magical. Everything is so French! Beautiful women, shimmering light, dark black coffee, flaky croissants. Everything is delicious. I fill myself with éclairs, savoring the rich creamy filling and slick drizzle of chocolate that I lick off my fingers.

I'm ready to be photographed with Brigit Bardot, but she is not available, so Daddy photographs Roger Vadim's *new* wife Annette, who is also gorgeous, with long blond hair that covers her breasts. I get her autograph.

In Brussels I receive a packet from my teacher, letters she made my classmates write. They're pretty much the same, "Dear Mary Lee, How is Europe. School is fun. See you soon." The handwriting and spelling is so bad. I take a red pen and correct it. Only my friend Kathie Gewirtz—whose name means spice!—has anything interesting to say about what she's doing. Like me, she loves to read, so she tells me all about the books she's reading.

I write a letter to the whole class, telling them about Blood Oranges, which I find disgusting, the parts of Germany that are still in ruins, the big statues of young men Hitler erected along the Autobahn, and nuns on bikes. I describe the big nuclear sculpture from the World's Fair and Island Markham where everyone wears wooden shoes. I don't tell them I'm homesick or that my grandmother's died. I try to be brave like Andy would want me to be.

The rest of the trip has its ups and downs: We buy Jo and Benjie a troll in Sweden, then take an overnight boat trip from Sweden to England. We get sunburned faces from lying wrapped in blankets on the deck, but it's the only way we don't feel seasick.

In England we meet Andy's younger brother, Bobs, who lives in a moldy 400-year old house. He has a white Sealyham terrier and a nineteen-year-old cat, who has had a hundred kittens. I'm horrified when Uncle Bobs tells me that each of the litters was put in a sack and drowned! I feel like I understand why Andy left this cold musty place where cats are routinely murdered. I feel closer to her than ever and can't believe she isn't waiting for us in Santa Monica.

Finally, it's June. In Liverpool my father makes arrangements to have our car shipped to the United States. When we take off at Heathrow Airport all I can think of is my own bed, my own room, my cats, waiting for me in Santa Monica.

We're met at the airport by Jo and Benjie, Pat and Charlie, Dale and Dell, everyone waving as we walk across the tarmac. Ann rides with Dell, Daddy with Dale, Mommy with the Becks and I in the back of Jo and Benjie's 1953 Chevy. Benjie smiles when I show him I still have the shell he gave me.

We pass the Santa Monica pier and drive along Ocean Avenue lined with palm trees. I roll down the window and breathe in the delicious smell of the Pacific Ocean. When we drive over our wooden bridge, I hear and smell the creek. I can't wait to pick and eat some spicy watercress. When I walk up the stairs into the house, it smells different, like no one opened the doors while we were gone. Some of the plants in the indoor planters look wilted. Mommy and Daddy talk to the people who stayed in the house as everyone else helps bring in our suitcases.

After a while Jo, Ben, Dale and the Becks leave. Ann and Dell go into her room. Mommy and Daddy go into the office and start looking through piles of mail. I go straight to the backyard and start calling the cats. After a while Mommy comes out.

"I'm absolutely furious," she says. "I don't think those people understood that the cats were supposed to be fed twice a day."

I stare at her. I don't get what she's trying to tell me.

"Mary Lee," she says, squatting down beside me. "I think the cats might have run away."

I look at her numbly. Cats don't just run away. They live where they're fed and petted, and loved.

"I'm sorry honey," she says putting her arms around me.

"I *knew* this would happen," I say. "It's all your fault. It's your fault Andy died and your fault the cats ran away." I push her away. "I hate you." I say and run into my room. My stuffy, empty room. My dolls stare down at me with dead eyes.

It's Wednesday, June 17th. The last day of school is Friday.

I spend the next two days sleeping, crying, yelling and throwing up. I'm not about to go to school and answer a bunch of stupid questions about my trip to Europe.

On Saturday the weather is warm so I go in the pool. On my back, staring at the sky, I feel like I'm floating on a cloud. Then I hear something. A meow? I turn over and dog paddle, looking up into the canyon and then I see her, Twitchy, coming down the hill with a kitten in her mouth.

I get out of the pool and stand dripping on the pavement as the cat approaches. I see two big bite marks on her back. She drops a tiny black kitten at my feet. It's skinny. Twitchy is skinny too.

"Mommy!" I call.

Then I sit down on the ground and hold the cat, burying my face in her fur. She smells like sumac and dry grass. She smells like home.

Chapter 7

NEIGHBORS

The Becks built their house the same year we built ours, 1955. Although they were our next door neighbors, you got to their house by a separate, long unpaved driveway with wild ginger growing on one side. You crossed the creek on a white painted bridge which they shared with another house.

My first memory of the Becks is during their home construction. I'm almost six, lying on my stomach in their front yard. Susie, my same age, is beside me. We're coloring. I'm careful to stay within the lines. Susie finds a stick of pink chalk and starts rubbing it on the rough paper. This is very upsetting and icky to me. Her eighteen-month old brother, in diapers, teeters toward us carrying a foot-long piece of rebar. He smacks me on the head. Susie laughs.

My parents were Democrats. The Becks were Republicans. But like my parents, Charlie worked at home, as a general contractor, at a big slanted drafting table in his office. He had been a pilot in WWII and flew jets for National Guard on weekends. He was medium height, with a tight physique and military haircut, quite good looking. His wife Pat was a little taller than him, and resembled Ava Gardner. She was outgoing and loved to laugh. Their house had a formal living room where kids weren't allowed, but also a big play room with a half-circle green couch we could run and jump on. Pat and the kids attended Corpus Christi Church in the Palisades and the kids went to Corpus Christi School.

Pat painted a big bull's eye on a white sheet and hung it on the hillside behind their carport for the kids to use as bow and arrow practice. Their front yard had a lawn and a big pool with a slide. Around the house ran a wide sidewalk for skating and bike riding. I hated skating, had no balance. When I was about ten, I thought the wide sidewalk would be a great place to play *Video Village*, a popular TV game show, hosted by Monty Hall in which contestants literally walked through the set.

Teresa, one year older than Susie and me, said she would be the MC. She put questions on 3" x 5" cards. I used different colored chalk to draw the squares on the pavement. I spent a month's allowance up at Newberry's Five and Ten Cent store on prizes. I guess our parents were busy because only Tim, age five, and Monty age four, agreed to be the audience. They sat crossed legged on the ground, eating popsicles.

Susie got all her answers right, so won all the prizes. Afterwards I asked if she felt like sharing them with me. She said no.

Susie collected chewed gum in a little set of plastic drawers her father had once used to hold nails, sorting the gum into green, pink, grey. She also collected Holy Cards and other relics such as a piece of the Pope's robe or a lock of a saint's hair. One day, painting our toenails in the kids' bathroom, Susie said, "I've promised myself to God. When I turn eighteen, I'm going to become a nun."

I thought this was quite noble of her and felt a pang of jealousy. The three of us had read a book about a nun who rescued Jewish children in WWII and "A Nun's Story" was one of our favorite movies.

Teresa had her mother's artistic skill and liked to draw. My mother was horrified by a realistic pencil drawing Teresa made of an eyeball factory—an eye moved along a conveyor belt, was pierced, the juices ran out, and it continued on, deflated till it fell over the edge into a bucket. When my mother saw it she called Pat and told her she found the images disturbing. But Pat laughed it off, saying Teresa had a vivid imagination. When Mother hung up, she muttered something under her breath about "bloodiness of those Catholics," and it was true, many of the stories of the saints told of their gruesome martyrdoms.

Teresa combed their dog Blacky's fur and twisted it into long threads which she knitted into a little blanket. She had a beautiful Japanese doll in a glass case. Both Susie and Teresa played the accordion and shared a pink bedroom with trundle beds, until Teresa turned twelve. Then her dad partitioned-off part of the playroom for her.

When Susie and I were seven and Teresa was eight, the little girl in the house next to theirs, Belinda, came over. Whereas we loved to dress up, sing, dance, run though the house yelling "sandstorm!" and dive under our sheet-capes, Belinda was small, dark and timid and we were never able to draw her out of herself. This day she came to tell us she was having a birthday party on Saturday. She was going to be six.

Mother took me to Pacific Palisades to buy Belinda's gift. At Newberry's I chose a miniature grocery store set, with tiny plastic cans of soup and peas, and little boxes of cereal and rice. I loved it. I wish I could have it for myself. We went across the street and I got to buy a pair of Easter shoes, white with ankle straps, and a pair of lace-trimmed white socks.

I was so excited about the party! I loved dressing up. Mother wrapped the gift and I carried it through the gate that connected our property to the Beck's. Their kitchen door was never locked, so I entered and called out.

Pat was behind the kitchen counter slicing a leg of lamb for sandwiches.

"Don't you look pretty?" she told me, "What's the occasion?"

"It's Belinda's birthday. Aren't Susie and Teresa ready?" Teresa heard my voice and came out of the bedroom. She was wearing pink shorts and a sleeveless shirt. "Why are you all dressed up?" she asked.

"Belinda's birthday party!" I said.

"Oh, yeah," she said, "I forgot." I followed her back into the bedroom. Susie was sitting on her bed, braiding her long brown hair. She too was dressed in shorts. When I told her why I was there she got up and started looking through their closet for something to take to the party. Then she remembered: her mother had accidentally washed a white wool sweater in hot water and shrunk it.

"This will fit Belinda," Susie said, holding up the tiny sweater.

While Teresa brushed her hair, I followed Susie into their mother's closet where she got a roll of wrapping paper to wrap up the sweater.

The three of us proceeded over to Belinda's house. We knocked on their kitchen door, waited, and pushed it open. The house was dark and dank. It smelled of mildew. Where were the balloons?

We walked through the house and found Belinda in her bedroom, playing with a Betsy McCall doll. She looked up surprised.

"We're here for your birthday party," Susie said. Belinda's mother came into the room, drying her hands with a dish towel.

"Belinda, why did you tell these girls you were having a birthday party?" her mother asked. Belinda would not look up from her doll. To us her mother said, "We took Belinda to Knott's Berry Farm yesterday. There is no party."

Teresa said, "Let's go back to our house and have a party." So we followed her. I carried the wrapped grocery store and Susie carried the wrapped sweater. I must have stepped in mud because when we sat down in Susie and Teresa's bathroom to share slices of bologna and water in Dixie cups, I saw that one of my new white shoes had a big brown blotch on it. Susie handed Belinda the package with the shrunken sweater. Belinda opened it and put it on. It fit.

I had dropped my package on Susie's bed before we went into the bathroom. Susie and Teresa didn't mention it. When someone suggested they go outside and ride their scooters, I said I wasn't dressed for it. I waited until they were outside to retrieve the grocery store and took it home with me.

Not long after that Belinda moved away and a new family moved in. They had two daughters, a son, and collie dogs. Tina and I would walk to and from the bus together throughout our elementary and junior high years. I don't know what became of Belinda.

Some of the happiest times of my childhood were spent with Mother and my friends. Daddy would be at the beach and we'd have the whole house all to ourselves. We'd sit at the dining room table and draw, or play Canasta, Scrabble or Life.

Or she would teach us "routines" we could do at a party. She was a good choreographer. We learned the time step, "shuffle off to Buffalo" and kick-ball-change. For "Peg of My Heart" we used parasols as props. We learned a "soft shoe" for "Up a Lazy River." Sue and Teresa had good voices and could sing harmony. I sang softly, smiled a lot and relied on my dancing skills.

When I was eleven, Mother taught us "Shanty in Old Shanty Town" which we would perform at an upcoming party. She made us each floor-length white dotted Swiss dresses with Peter Pan collars and green satin cummerbunds. We looked fantastic, like the Lennon sisters. I'm sad that I can't find any photographs of that party or us in our pretty dresses.

DAYS OF DRESSES

I want to go back to the days of dresses
when men wore hats
ironed shirts, pleated slacks
and shiny shoes
that clicked on the pavement.

I remember shopping for fabric with my mother,
walking down wooden aisles of colored cloth,
feeling between my fingers flannel, muslin, linen,
corduroy and cotton, seersucker and dotted Swiss.

Saleswomen in high heeled pumps,
pressed blouses and straight skirts
would carry our huge bolt
and thump it like a carcass
on the giant table
then un-spool it
—thwack, thwack, thwack—
before cutting our portion precisely
with scalloped pinking shears.

I loved picking out zippers and buttons and thread
in rainbows of colors, and once
a creamy green lining
to shield me from scratchy wool.

I remember how once, after shopping
at the Fabric Store, mother got me
and Susie and Teresa to sing to the attendant
"Thank you, thank you very much
we're so glad we could park in your lot!"
to the tune of "I've Told Every Little Star"
in three part harmony.

At home Mother cleared the dining room table,
unfolded the cloth and expertly
pinned the sheer paper pattern like a puzzle,
so as not to waste.
She used only special stainless steel shears,
that sliced through the cloth
like a sailboat slices the sea.

Then she'd pin each portion onto me,
as I stood stock-still, arms outstretched:
bodice, then skirt, then sleeves.

My favorite dress was red and white
stripped cotton, short sleeves, v-neck,
v-waist, full skirt and best of all
a big bow that tied in back.

I was so beautiful in that dress, no one
noticed my missing tooth or skinny legs.
Around the hem, red rick-rack completed
the impression that I was a girl
worthy of a mother's attention,
her patience, skill and concentration.
My petticoat rustled a mother's love.

Mother was also a natural storyteller. One hot summer day, my friends and I had gone swimming in our pool, and were lying on the hot pavement, drying off. Mother sat on the ground with us and started to tell us a story about bees.

"Do you hear that buzzing?" she asked. We all strained to hear. I could hear a faint breeze rustling the oak leaves and if I held my breath, the distant ocean, a soft, dull thud every few seconds. But no bees.

"I do!" Susie cried. So I listened harder. Mother proceeded to tell a story about a magic hive that lived deep within the ancient oak on the hill. Half-way through her story the phone rang.

"Don't answer it!" I pleaded. But these were the days before answering machines, so Mother got up and went inside. Indeed, it was a business call and she wasn't able to return to finish the story.

"Let's make taffy," Teresa suggested.

"Okay," I said, sitting up. I went into the shady house, past Mother on the kitchen phone, and found a bag of marshmallows in the pantry. I brought the bag and a box of wax paper outside. I tore off a sheet for each of us. Then we all took a marshmallow and started to knead it between our fingers until it was sticky, the consistency of taffy. We placed each little mound of the wax paper, until we had three apiece.

"A bee!" Susie shouted and sure enough a honey bee had landed on one of her candies. "Shoo!" she said and waved it away. Quickly she folded her wax paper so it covered the marshmallow confections.

Teresa opened the door for me so I could carry our work inside. I set the stack on the counter and opened the freezer, then set them inside. It would take a few hours for them to harden.

"Shrimp!" I exclaimed when I saw that Mother had bought my favorite Swanson's TV Dinner. This was a special treat I would eat when she and Daddy went out to dinner without me.

When we first moved into our Hightree house I used to throw fits when they'd go out without me. I was jealous when they went to the Chatham in Westwood, a dim restaurant with red leather booths. They served spaghetti with meat sauce, topped by thin slivers of turkey. Yum.

But now that I was getting older I looked forward to nights when my parents went out. The Becks continually asked me to spend the night but inevitably I'd get up and come home at bedtime. I liked playing with them and loved their mom's cooking. Sometimes on Friday nights she made pancakes and poured them into all sorts of shapes, guitars or Mickey Mouse. But after we'd eaten and played some board games I wanted to go home to my own bed and my cat.

When the Becks planned a camp out on the other side of the creek, my father brought over a chaise lounge for me, because he knew I had no desire to sleep on the hard ground. Even with this luxury I went home at 9 o'clock, and returned in the morning to drink hot chocolate with everyone else, as the sun came up.

Susie, Teresa and I liked to comb our hair in their parents' big bathroom, where all three of us could stand side-by-side and primp at the same time.

One day Susie mused aloud, "Being blond is ok. You can pretend to be Swedish or English. But being brunette is so much better. I can be Spanish, or Japanese, or Chinese, or Colombian . . ." Her voice trailed off in a way that let me know she felt sorry for me.

When I was nine, Mother got the idea to take pictures of me, Susie and Teresa, dressed up as movie stars. "I bet if we take really good pictures, we can sell an article to *Life* magazine," she said.

What a great idea! The year before she had taken pictures of me as Eloise and sent them in to a casting director, but Evelyn Rudy got the part in the movie.

Mother looked at each of us and decided that Susie and Teresa looked Italian. "Gina Lollabrigida and Sophia Loren," she said and we followed her into the dressing room.

Inside the closet my father had built a tall dresser with drawers. In several of them he'd made dividers to hold bathing suits. Susie, Teresa and I loved to play "Miss Universe" and walk back and forth through the house in high heels and bathing suits. We'd often play more than one contestant, just to make it last longer. We were practicing for when we were older and would be real bathing beauties, walking in heels, waving to the crowd, answering questions about how we would make the world a better place.

We also had fun making ourselves look ugly, which we thought was funny. Over the years so many "poor girls" as my mother called them, would show up with their "agents" (boyfriends) who thought they had the makings of a model. A lot of the girls were extremely shy. Some wore way too much make up. Others were just plain homely. Most of the men who bought my father's first bestselling book, *How to Photograph Women,* thought if they used the right techniques they could make their girlfriends look like Kim Novak. Instead of having compassion for these young women, my friends and I made fun of them.

We dressed up in dowdy baggy clothes and messed up our hair. We smeared lipstick messily over our mouths and drew ridiculous eyebrows. We went outside through my bedroom and rang the doorbell. When my father answered we said, in a nasal voice, "We want to be *maaadels.* Will you take our *pik-sha?*" Of course, he did.

But this time we really would be glamorous. What Mother couldn't find in the dressing room, Pat supplemented from her wardrobe: full long skirts, off-the shoulder blouses. Susie got to wear a tortoise-shell comb and drape a lace *mantilla* over it, just like a real Spanish *señorita.*

Mother decided I would be Marilyn Monroe. She made me a tight white satin dress with a mesh flounce. I already had plastic high heels I'd bought with my allowance, at Newberry's. When it was my turn, I posed in the studio, making Marilyn's classis face by saying "oooohhh."

The pictures turned out great, but *Life* didn't publish the story. Perhaps the editors thought it was improper for pre-pubescent girls to look so sexy.

Another favorite activity was to play store. I would price and lay out items on my long white chest of drawers. Susie, Teresa and Tina would come over and shop. One day Susie bought a bracelet for five cents. It had a series of small colored stones hanging from it. Susie gave me a nickel and I helped her put it on her wrist.

It was late in the afternoon, time to clean up. I opened a drawer and put the unsold items carefully inside.

"I really like this bracelet!" Susie said.

"Good," I said.

"Are you sure you want to sell it?" she asked. "It's really cute. And it goes with a lot of stuff." She extended her arm and wiggled her wrist so light played on the stones.

"I don't wear it very often," I said, admiring it on her.

"But you should!" Susie said, "It's really pretty. I'll sell it back to you if you want." I thought about it and realized that she might be right. It was a pretty bracelet.

"Okay," I said.

"Ten cents," Susie answered. And so I got my bracelet back and Susie made five cents.

One day, when we were eleven, Susie and I were walking up the street, on our way to Rustic Canyon Park. They had a vending machine that sold warm cans of chili and baked beans for twenty-five cents. This was a perfect snack for hungry girls who had spent all day in the pool.

About half-way up the street, I spotted something orange in a vacant lot. "What's that?" I asked Susie. She stopped and squinted.

"Let's go look," she replied. We discovered that it was an axle and wagon wheels, about four-feet high. What a treasure!

"Let's take it to my house!" I suggested. So together we extricated it from the weeds and dragged it into the street. We decided to push, rather than pull it. It almost got away from us when we came to the steep slope of our driveway but the momentum helped carry it up the big dip and over the bridge, where it rattled wonderfully on the wood.

By the time we got it home I knew what I wanted to do with it.

"Let's make a traveling store!" I said to Susie. She thought it sounded like fun.

My dad was in the office, standing in front of the light box, looking at color transparencies.

"Daddy! You'll never believe what we found!" I said, taking him by the hand. "Come outside!" My mind was racing. I dragged him outside. He admired our find.

"I want to make a traveling store, Daddy, can you help us?"

He was quiet for a minute, then said, "Go get a pencil and paper." I ran back into the house. When I came back with the pencil and paper I saw he was measuring with his big metal tape measure. He called out numbers and I wrote them down.

"Would you like a rack, to hang clothes?" he asked.

"Yes!" I said, "That would be great. I'm thinking we can use the wicker laundry basket for shoes . . ."

By the next day Daddy had constructed a plywood platform, with a lip around it so our things wouldn't fall off. He used pipes to make a clothes rack. At the dining room table I worked on a poster: TRAVELING STORE in black Marks-a-lot, and all around it pictures and words: shoes, toys, cosmetics, kitchen utensils, dolls, records.

Susie and Teresa brought bags of items from their house and I contributed what I had been saving up for my next bedroom store, but it didn't look like much.

"I know!" I said, "Let's go around the neighborhood and collect donations!" This turned out to be an excellent idea.

On Friday, Susie, Teresa and I took the cart through the neighborhood—Hightree and Brooktree but not as far as Sunset Boulevard—and collected all sorts of stuff. One woman gave us six half-used Apple Red lipsticks. We got a flour sifter, rolling pin, several pairs of men's shoes, rubber boots, at least five dolls, a slinky, two hula hoops, an Etch-a-Sketch and three eggs of Silly Putty. I donated my powder blue car coat and hung it on the rack along with a beaded sweater, tee-shirts, slacks, skirts and an old pink bathrobe. I had so much fun sorting. To save time I made up a price list instead of individually pricing each item.

The next day we went back through the neighborhood offering up our goods. Unfortunately we only sold about a third of the items. We felt discouraged, returning home, but then I got the idea that we should take the cart up to the park.

"But not today," Teresa said, "I want to go swimming."

"Me too," I told her. "But, tomorrow, let's do it."

"After church," Susie said.

As we neared the end of our street we saw their cousin Patrick coming toward us.

Oh no, I thought. He better not want to get in on the action. The agreement was that we would split everything three ways. We didn't want to share with him and we didn't need his help.

"Hey!" he called.

"Hi Patrick," Susie said and we kept walking past him.

"Let me help you!" he said and tried to wrestle the cart away from us. Just as we arrived at the mailboxes—I don't know how it happened—the cart took off on its own, down the steep driveway. We couldn't catch it in time to steer it over the bridge. It careened down toward the Overpeck's garage and turned over.

I wanted to kill him. Instead I walked to the house and brought my dad back with his Roleiflex. He had started a roll of film, documenting how the Traveling Store was made. I figured he might as well include this fiasco.

Only two bottles of perfume were broken. The rest of the things survived. We put everything back and parked the Traveling Store at my house then went next door and spent several hours in the Beck's pool.

The next day we took the cart up to the park and within two hours we had sold almost everything, making $30.00 which we split three ways. My mother took what was left to the Good Will. I wish my dad were alive to ask if he remembered what became of that mysterious set of wagon wheels that became The Traveling Store.

The Becks had a small concrete Buddha in their front yard. I had access to a blue Japanese kimono and a black Chinese robe with orange silk dragons that my father's Uncle had sent us from Asia. These inspired me to write *The Missing Eye*, a three-page typed play starring me, Susie and Teresa. We would perform it on the hill in my back yard.

We learned our lines and I blocked the action. I made up invitations and put them in all the mailboxes on Hightree Road. The Saturday morning of the play, I set up chairs in our back yard and asked Mother to make some popcorn, which I intended to sell to the audience.

Susie and Teresa came over and told me they couldn't do the play, they were going to P.O.P.—Pacific Ocean Park. They asked if I wanted to go with them. I said no. I carried the chairs back into the house. I took the big pot of popcorn and threw it over the bank of the creek, for the birds. I was madder than I had ever been at my two best friends. I spent the rest of the day in my room with my cat, reading.

But I never stayed mad at my friends for long. There was too much fun stuff to do, whether at my house dressing up, or their house sliding into the pool, or finding pollywogs in the creek. We were ever active, curious, and never bored.

Chapter 8

MY OWN GOOD PRISONER

When fifth grade started in the fall of 1959 I had been out of school for six months: first our three-month trip to Europe, then summer vacation. My report card from that semester records that I was absent half the days. I just didn't want to go to school. I had so much to do at home: read, write, play with my friends, watch *The Thin Man* on TV—I loved their dog, Asta—observe my parents working, talk to their employees, find things to look at under my microscope . . . In comparison, school was boring.

My parents and sister were extremely allergic to poison oak. But I was immune. When I didn't want to go to school, I could hide up in the canyon and no one could come after me.

GIRL CHILD

I was born with little tiny teeth beneath my gums,
small monkey hands, wisps of hair and
veins across my skull.
I was red and wrinkled with a bitter expression.

Within ten years I stretched out, grew pale, then tan,
my hair went from dark to blond to a shimmer-y greenish hue
from swimming all summer in chlorinated pools.

My hearing was acute.
I learned to be aloof.

I hid in the deep ivied canyon
where water seeped all year long
and the heavy air smelled like moss.

I developed an appreciation
for the leathery texture of sprawling oaks,
their mean little leaves formed a ragged screen
where I was protected from words and lack of kisses.

I'd crawl through openings in red sumac
following tracks to dead end dens, littered with feathers.

Or I'd trace the spring to its boggy trickle
and squat for hours in my black galoshes
like a rock
like a ghost
like a toad.

I once picked a sprig of poison oak and stuck it in a pot of dirt.
When my mother knocked on my bedroom door and said it was
time to go to school, I opened the door, and held the pot in front of

me, the way one holds a cross up to a vampire. She had no option but to throw her hands up in disgust and leave me be.

Sometimes, on days when my mother's will was stronger than mine and she won, I would go to the nurse's office and say I didn't feel well. I had the benefit of chronic swollen glands to back me up. After a while I felt that the nurse's room, off the attendance office, was my private haven.

MY OWN GOOD PRISONER

When I was ten
I got good at
lying still for hours
counting dots on the ceiling
in my own little cubicle
in the nurse's office.

I wasn't really sick.
But I needed to be removed
from shrieking children
on the playground
boys in black shoes
flinging rubber balls
at girls in skirts.

I enjoyed the muffled voice
of the school secretary, occasional
visits from the janitor
come to dust.
I liked the way
the phone rang
and was promptly
answered.

I belonged in an office.
I was born in an office.

I'd fall asleep to my mother's typing,
the roll of paper in the plenum
the sweet smack of the keys
the jaunty bell at the end of the line
the flick of her wrist on the carriage return,
the final period. Then
the paper pulled out in one crisp snap
to be signed, folded and mailed.

Outside on the playground
kids screamed and ran
poked and jabbed each other
told mean jokes
made each other cry.

I was insulated
by wire windows
safe on my narrow cot
my own good prisoner
reluctantly released at three o'clock.

I'd wait till the buses were loaded
to begin my journey home.

The ugly yellow container
grunted up the hill
filled with smug, flushed faces
that gawked at me
like I was a stuck-up movie star
too famous to give autographs.

One very hot day I debated whether I should get on the bus. But I didn't want to answer questions about where I had been all day. So I went to the girls' bathroom and waited until I heard the busses lumbering up the hill. Then I set out to walk home.

I took Mesa Road. My throat was so parched. I imagined I was stranded in a desert, trying to find water. I carried my lunch sack but there was nothing to drink it in, just Graham crackers and a tuna sandwich. I had drunk my apple juice at lunchtime. I thought maybe eating a cracker would produce saliva.

I leaned against a garden wall and opened the brown paper bag. I took out a cracker. I bit into it. Some spit was generated but not enough to make swallowing easy. I was thirsty and hungry. But I knew *many* people in the world were starving. This must be what it felt like.

When I reached Latimer Road, shade protected me from the beating sun. Passing the park I heard the thwack of tennis balls against rackets. I passed Lee Marvin's walled home, and the dark-shingled house with camel hair grass growing in bumpy clumps. I turned left on Brooktree then left again on Hightree. The walk became easier as the road descended.

Finally I arrived at our bridge. The sweet smell of the creek filled my lungs and brought me back to life. I opened the front door and I heard voices in the studio. I walked in and slid open the shoji screen door. I stood there, not saying anything. All eyes turned to me. Mother's mouth dropped open.

"I didn't eat all day, and I walked all the way home," I said. My mother and father looked at each other. Dramatically I turned. I dropped my lunch sack on the kitchen counter and went into my room.

A few minutes later Mother opened my door. "I've made you some soup," she said.

I sat at the kitchen counter and slowly savored a delicious bowl of Campbell's Bean with Bacon soup—so salty, so good.

Another time, when I knew our car was in the shop for repairs, I decided to eat breakfast but not get dressed. Mother confronted me in the kitchen.

"You're not sick, Mary Lee," she said. "You're going to school today."

"It's too late," I said calmly. "The bus has already left."

"Get dressed!" she yelled. "You're going to school if I have to walk you there myself!"

My father hated our confrontations. When I was in first grade, I used to run home from the bus stop before the bus arrived. I didn't like Mrs. Real, our teacher. She had huge bags under her eyes and wore a long shapeless dress. She reminded me of the mean women at the orphanage on *The Little Rascals*. She tried to make me learn how to "run in" at jump rope. I didn't mind starting from standing still and saying, "go!" to the two girls holding the long white rope. But running in never worked. Especially when it was Double Dutch.

On the day I ran back home, Mother drove me to school. The next morning my father took my hand and marched me to the bus stop. He stayed with me until the bus came, then carried me on to the bus, kicking and screaming.

This time he just gave me a look that said *You've brought this on yourself.*

Reluctantly I got dressed. Mother took my hand and together we walked the mile to school. The school secretary stood up when we walked in. "I'm sorry we're late," Mother said.

"I have a temperature!" I insisted. "I wanted to stay home but she made me walk all the way!"

Mother pressed her fingers to her eyes. Years later I would find her diary from this year with an entry that said, *Why is Mary Lee torturing me?*

The principal came out of her office. The three women looked at each other.

"I have a temperature," I repeated.

The secretary came around the counter and led me into the nurse's room. The nurse gave me a sympathetic smile. She shook out a thermometer and stuck it under my tongue. I could hear Mother talking to the principal as the nurse stared at her watch.

In three minutes the nurse removed the thermometer and looked at it. "Stay here, Mary Lee," she said.

I stretched out on "my" cot as she and the secretary went back out to the office. I strained to hear what they were saying but couldn't quite make it out.

Then I heard my mother ask, "May I use your phone?"

Fifteen minutes later Dale, my parent's assistant, arrived to take us home. I sat in the back of his big white Lincoln Continental and enjoyed the smooth ride back up the hill.

Dr. Evelyn Troup, child psychologist saved our family. I don't know how my mother found her, perhaps the principal recommended her. Dr. Troup was a tiny woman, in her mid-fifties, with crippling rheumatoid arthritis. Her hands were deformed and she stooped. But I loved her.

In her office she had a tiny refrigerator. The first thing she did when we were alone together was let me pick out what I wanted to drink. She had little bottles of Welch's Grape Juice and cans of apple, pineapple and orange juice. Over the course of our four sessions I chose a different drink each week. Although they were exactly what my mother put in my lunch, they tasted way better, because they were *cold*.

Dr. Troup had dolls and stuffed animals. She let me draw and color. While I played, we talked. I enjoyed it. I felt sad when she told me I didn't need to come anymore.

Her diagnosis: I was bored at school. She recommended that I take accelerated classes and engage in extracurricular activities. Mother enrolled me in an after-school French class which was a great idea. What could be more fun than pretending to be French and just talking? The teacher gave each of us a French name. Unfortunately for me she chose Claude, which sounded like *clod*, a clump of dirt. Otherwise I loved it.

Years later mother told me Dr. Troup also prescribed "little white pills." After I had taken them for a few weeks everyone saw a remarkable change in me. I was more outgoing and cheerful. My appetite improved. I wonder what sort of drugs doctors prescribed back then for a bored ten-year-old girl. Hormones?

I only took the pills for a short time. Something else happened in the spring of 1960: boys finally started to notice me.

Chapter 9

THE AWKWARD YEARS

Happy Holidays!

"It's not the quantity of meat, it's cheerful hearts that make the feast . . . ."

By the time I graduated from Canyon Elementary School in 1961, I'd come to like school again. I adored Miss Gale (Beverly), our twenty-two-year-old sixth-grade teacher. She looked and dressed like Jackie Kennedy, with perfect poofy brown hair, cat's eye glasses and pencil skirts. At the beginning of the school year she changed her nail polish everyday to match her outfits but by November this time-consuming ritual had been abandoned.

One day she got so exasperated with Jeff Flitterman, a toe-head blond wise guy, that she put her head down on her desk and cried. The boys stifled their giggles as Jeff took his punishment, sauntering smugly to the cloak room. But we girls gave him nasty looks. After school, waiting for the bus, I confronted him.

"Why do you have to be such a jerk?" I said.

"Ah, shut up!" he said and turned to walk away. I grabbed for his arm but he pulled away and my fingernail scraped down his forearm. Just as I started to say I was sorry, he hauled off and socked me in the stomach. I doubled over, coughing. Girlfriends gathered around, patting me on the back and picking up my spilled books.

I had a huge crush on Mr. Fox, the after school playground coach. He wore cool dark glasses like Kooky on *77 Sunset Strip*. Although I had never been athletic—in third grade I used to sing "Cry Me a River" for kids waiting on the bench for tetherball, instead of playing that sadistic game—I stayed after school just to hang around "Dicky," as we called him.

My classroom was connected to the other sixth-grade class by the cloak room. I'd use any excuse to "run errands" for Miss Gale so that I could visit Kathie in the other room. At lunchtime we all got to be together again. But sometimes that was just too long to wait.

When the lunch bell rang, a group of my friends and I would follow Miss Gale to the cafeteria. We wanted to hear all about her boyfriend, Bill. She'd tolerantly say, "I'll see you after lunch!" as she entered the Teachers' Lounge.

We also liked the cafeteria ladies who made a few extra "teacher's salads" for us—decent-sized portions of lettuce, carrots, cucumber and tomatoes, not the few teaspoons of greens in the kids' version. Even then we thought about our health.

By sixth grade I packed my own lunch the night before—a Wheat Berry bread sandwich of white albacore tuna, or turkey, sometimes roast beef, with lettuce and tomato, a small can of apple juice and one Van de Camp cookie, chocolate-chip cookie, cherry shortbread or oatmeal raisin. I'd supplement this with the cold, crunchy salad.

I must admit, though, that once in a while I'd trade sandwiches with Marilyn.

The tuna in her sandwiches was a brilliant orange and the Wonder Bread was like nothing I'd ever eaten, soft, white, chewy. Sometimes I'd press the sandwich between my hands to see how flat I could make it. The bizarre texture and taste seemed something astronauts would eat.

One night, preparing my lunch for the next day, I smelled something funny. I opened a cabinet under the counter that we hardly ever used, and pulled out a glass dish full of lumps and mounds of multi-colored mold. A forgotten pie! I set it on the counter and picked up the phone.

"Kathie!" I cried when she answered, "I found my science project!"

It smelled so bad my mother made me keep it in the garage overnight. I got out the M volume of Encyclopedia Britannica and wrote a report on mold. My dad drove me to school the next day. I got an A.

I loved typing school reports on Mother's old Royal typewriter. They looked so professional. However, it meant less pages than a handwritten report. So, I'd supplement with pictures cut out of *National Geographic, Life* and *Look*. Sometimes I'd even find photographs in *Popular Photography* or *Mechanics Illustrated*—my parents subscribed to a *lot* of magazines.

Mother taught me how to type a title page: you'd count the number of spaces in your title and divide it by two, then starting in the middle of the page—a very light fold—you had to backspace the right amount of spaces. I loved doing this. I'd type, *Various Types of Food Mold* on one line, *by* several lines down and *Mary Lee Gowland* last. Even then I loved seeing my name in print.

Kathie and another friend had an on-going contest to see who could make the longest report. One year their parents had to drive them to school, the reports were so big. They got a roll-cart from the office and took it to the curb, where they loaded their foot-high reports. Teachers hadn't stipulated a maximum number of pages so they'd pasted one little picture on each page and had only three or four pages of actual text. I believe they got A minuses.

By my twelfth birthday, in May 1961, my hair had grown to my shoulders and turned up in a natural "flip." I had bangs and often wore a Pixie Band, an elasticized headband that came in a variety of colors. My favorite outfit was a dark jumper worn with a white, puff-sleeved blouse, and white apron. I thought it made me look like a German *fraulein,* with a waist and bustline.

I never did grow into the size six, red patent-leather flats Mother had bought me the fall before. By now I shopped at Vin Baker, my favorite women's shoe store on the Third Street mall. There I bought what I called my "pilgrim shoes"—pointed black flats with a big buckle. When boys got too sassy I'd kick them in the shins.

The only problem was my teeth. I had such a narrow mouth. My two huge front teeth fought for space pushing my eye teeth up, making me feel like a monster. I'd need braces, come fall.

For sixth-grade graduation Mother made me a stylish dress of raw silk. The square-neck bodice was half turquoise and half white. The full skirt had the same colors on opposite sides. At the waist I wore a turquoise cummerbund. The most exciting part was that I got to buy my first pair of heels, pointed white pumps. The heels were only one inch high, but wearing them made me feel very grown up. I felt sorry for the girls whose mothers made them wear flats.

The same year I graduated from elementary to junior high school, my sister Ann graduated from University High School and would be going to Santa Monica City College City in the fall. She and some girlfriends rented an apartment in West L.A. As soon as she moved out, I moved into her room at the front of the house and got out of the middle bedroom which I never liked. I was glad that I'd no longer have to hear my parents talking—or arguing—on the other side of my bedroom wall.

Paul Revere Junior High School was seven miles east, past the Riviera Country Club, walking distance from Kathie's house, but not mine. The bus picked us up at Sunset Boulevard. On it were kids from Marquez Elementary, the private Episcopal school, and Catholic Corpus Christi. At school we'd be thrown in with kids from Kenter Canyon and Bellagio. We Canyon kids stuck together in the midst of all this newness.

For a long time I missed the wonderful library at Canyon that had been the original one-room school built in 1894, the year my grandmother Andy was born. There, on lunch break, I first read Hugh Lofting's *Doctor Doolittle* books. I savored *The Incredible Journey*, about a cat and two dogs that make a cross-country trip to find their owners. And in that sweet little building, I checked out Albert Peyson Terhune's *Lad a Dog* (1919), *The Way of the Dog* (1932) and my favorite, *Wolf* (1925). I remember asking my mother if I could record the last chapter on our big reel-to-reel tape recorder. I'll never forget the last line. The dog Wolf has been killed, performing some heroic act. *"And still, people will say, he died like a dog."* I could barely get the words out, I was so choked up. I'm sure that my love of animals comes not only from having cats when I was young, but from reading these wonderful writers.

A month after graduation I got my period. Mother showed me how to attach the bulky Kotex pad to an elastic belt. I thought for sure everyone could see it, so when "George" came to visit, I'd wear my blue moo moo, which mother had helped me sew. I learned to put a G on the calendar each month and could anticipate when the messy, embarrassing and eventually painful experience would come again. My cycles were five weeks instead of four.

In fifth grade Mother had bought me a "training bra" which had soft stretchy cups. I remember one day some neighborhood kids came over and invited me to go bike riding. I was peddling along when it dawned on me that the boy in back of me might see my bra through my white shirt. I slowed down and let him pass. From then on, I made sure that I only wore dark clothes that would not betray my secret.

Shortly after sixth-grade graduation, Susie, Teresa and I went shopping for bathing suits at J.C. Penny, on the corner of Wilshire and Third Street. We took the terrazzo stairs to the second floor. I'd been wearing a red, rubbery one-piece that was so uncomfortable when sand got trapped inside it.

I found a darling two piece made of black and white "ticking" The bottom was a modest bikini, just below the navel, with a woven belt. What I really liked about it was that the top was a halter, so I could wear a bra under it. Even then I was developing the sort of breasts that "showed" through clothes. Until 1970, when I considered myself "feminist" and threw out all my bras, I did everything I could to make my breasts inconspicuous.

The only problem, I discovered, was when I laid on my back on my beach towel. I was so thin that my hip bones stuck up. What if boys could peer down the gap between my abdomen and my suit and see? It seemed there was always something to be embarrassed about.

One day in July, Kathie and I went next door to Susie and Teresa's house and found their mom, Pat. trimming their hair. She was an artist, after all, and on the cutting edge of fashion. Kathie and I decided we wanted Pat to cut our hair, too. We all wanted to look alike and thought shorter hair would make us look more sophisticated. Kathie, Susie and Teresa, were brunettes, like Connie Francis and I, the blond, wanted to look like Connie Stevens.

I took pictures of us with my Instamatic, front, side and back. Junior High School, here we come!

That night my mother got a call from Kathie's grandmother who ranted on and on, furious that her granddaughter's tresses had been cut without permission. Mother politely said that we all looked adorable, and besides snort hair was much easier to care for. When Kathie's grandmother wouldn't stop griping, Mother said, "It'll grow back!"

When school started I learned where my classes were and which friends would be with me. We Canyon kids established ourselves in one corner of the lunch area. Within a few weeks some girls had formed a club called the LaMours. I wasn't invited in. But by ninth grade, it evolved into the Duprees, a YWCA sponsored service club, and I was voted in.

I'd had crushes on boys since first grade but had never had a boyfriend. I hoped this would change in Junior High. Unfortunately, the kind of attention I got was not what I wanted.

Two brothers lived at the end of our street, so we rode the same bus to school. Mornings they left me alone, but in the afternoon, when we got off the bus, the Helms Bakery truck would be waiting. One day the boys bought an extra jelly donut and threw it at my back. They burst out laughing as the purple mess left a big splotch on my white blouse.

I was furious, of course, and told my mother. She called their parents. The next day I tried to hang back and let them go ahead of us, but they stood with some of their other buddies, acting like they were discussing something important. My friend Tina said, "Come on," and so we started down toward Hightree.

Soon we heard footsteps behind us and then I was propelled forward—one of the brothers had stepped on the back of my shoe, making me stumble.

Again, I told my mother. This time she went over to their house to talk to the boys' parents. The next day the brothers flipped my books. (Before book bags, we clutched our binder and books close to our chests.) I was so furious I started yelling at them but they ran on ahead shouting, "Sorry Hairy Lee!"

HAIRY LEE

When I was twelve
the boys called me "Hairy Lee"

My thin tan legs were covered
in golden down, fine as chick feathers.

I wanted to be a *chick* chick, a teenager.
I liked boys and wanted them to like me.

One night when my parents were at a party
I snuck into their bathroom.

I stuck my foot in my father's sink
and shaved.

My cool white sheets were exquisitely smooth
on my sensitive skin, so bare.

Except for the spots covered in Band-aids
where I'd nicked myself and bled.

Later that fall I got braces, a torment that would last until I was fifteen. Dr. Ricketts and Dr. Bench shared an office in the Palisades. They determined that I should start with a retainer to widen my palate. I actually still have those first impressions. It's strange what we keep over the years.

The memory of that oozing pink goo being pressed into the roof of my mouth is as vivid as if it happened yesterday. Oh, how I'd gag, trying to stay calm and breathe through my nose. Little did I realize this was just the beginning of the torture. On the next visit a hard split-palate retainer was clamped into the roof of my mouth. I was instructed to inserted a "key" into a cog in the middle, every night, and rotate it one click. This increased the pressure.

I went to the orthodontist every other week. On one visit Dr. Ricketts looked at my mouth and said, "Continue to make one turn per night."

Then the next time I went Dr. Bench said, "Oh, no, that's too much!" and told me to loosen it over a period of days.

The next time I went, Dr. Ricketts said, "What happened?" and began to tighten it. Dr. Bench came in. They stood over me arguing. Dr. Rickets dropped his instruments onto my chest as he worked, hitting me in the sternum, coming much too close to my tender breasts.

Eventually I got full bands on my top and bottom teeth, and tiny rubber bands that linked the top of my mouth to the lower jaw. My jaw and mouth always hurt. I learned to cut corn off the cob and never bite directly into anything, such as an apple or sandwich. I'd cut fruit into little pieces, and rip my sandwich into bite sized morsels. I didn't want to be like some kids who didn't notice when food got stuck in their braces. Gross.

Speaking of food, my father had been eating yogurt for years—plain Yami yogurt that he'd buy at the health food store next to the Lyle Fox Gym in the Palisades. At Kathie's house we'd eat yogurt with grape juice and wheat germ. Yummy. We were thrilled when Dannon came out with individual servings of strawberry yogurt in the early 60s and it became a healthy staple.

I'm amazed that in junior high school I'd eat a poached egg on an English muffin and hot chocolate for breakfast, a sweet sticky bun at "nutrition," a hearty cafeteria lunch, then walk the steep hill to the Brentwood Country Club on San Vicente after school, for a hamburger, fries and some fresh squeezed carrot juice, and *still* have room for dinner. And yet, it wasn't until high school that I weighed a hundred pounds.

THE ORANGE SWEATER

When I was thirteen
what I wanted more than anything
was a mohair sweater, bright as a blood orange,
a huge cocoon to cover my skinny frame
protect me, make me appear
bigger than I was.
I remember the feel, plush
like nothing in our house of glass and terrazzo
every surface sleek Danish Modern, white and beige.
The sweater was magnificent.
The fibers retained a wild animal vibration
split hooves, eerie green eyes,
curved horns like a cornucopia.
I knew goats loved to climb
the way I loved to climb into the canyon
by myself and hear nothing
but my heart
and the trickle of springs.
The enormous orange sweater
blanketed my skinny arms
my small sore breasts.
The cable-knit pattern
would bind me until
I was old enough
to emerge into womanhood
and no longer need
to hide.

I liked having a variety of teachers. I remember being flattered the day Miss Katz, an English teacher said my hairdo was never the same two days in a row. Mr. Jones was considered a "letch" because he placed the pretty girls in the front row. But he got away with it because he reminded us of Sean Connery, who had just played James Bond. My pretty female math teacher drove the boys crazy. She'd sit on the edge of her desk and rub lotion into her legs. I remember her commenting on her hand writing. "Oh, I must be feeling happy today," when the writing tilted up. Junior high was like living in an encyclopedia, I learned so much every day.

I learned the population of the United States was 185 million people. I learned that some of the boys I had crushes on were smart, but rebellious and had to be in S.A., "social adjustment" class.

Eventually my mother put me in accelerated classes which were even more interesting. Between what I learned academically at school, dances my girlfriends and I learned watching American Bandstand, and lyrics picked up listening to the radio, my life had become one new, exciting experience after another. If only I had a boyfriend!

But who would fall in love with me, a girl with braces, five-foot-three, weighing only eighty-seven pounds?

Chapter 10

STATE BEACH

State Beach was a state of mind. Only one city block long, it was our refuge from the city where we went for different reasons at different times in our lives: to socialize, to exercise, or to walk alone with a broken heart. Nestled in the curve of Santa Monica Bay, bordered on the north by the Malibu Mountains and on the south by the Palos Verdes Peninsula, it was cool and spacious, an escape from the concrete city: no trees, no grass, no picnic tables—just sand, and sky, and water reaching all the way to China.

Wasn't it our religion, to sit stock still and face west, limp and relaxed, faces upturned, almost prayerful, calm? We knew the sun had healing powers so we soaked it up, day after day, first on our backs, then on our stomachs like supplicants, passive, and obedient.

When we got hot, we sat up and squinted into the dazzling light of sun on water and sun in the air. We stood and stretched, inhaled and exhaled, then made our way through undulating sand, careful to avoid bits of glass, and bits of charcoal, and lumps of gum and old cigarettes.

We entered the ocean solemnly. The soles of our feet were first to feel the wet sand's tingle, then foam around our ankles, like a blessing, vibrant and churning and our minds came alive. Some of us paused to splash the sparkling water on sun-warmed skin, but others plunged ahead like warriors to battle, neither gasping nor pausing in the tumultuous tide.

The secret was to go beyond the breakers, to plow through quickly in one quick burst, slice the wave and emerge behind it into calmness and vastness, into nothing but green.

Huge brown pelicans swooped so low you could almost touch them as they glided over us on enormous wings. Looking west toward China we felt the hugeness of the ocean—its depth, its width—and the volume of water with its currents and creatures and coral and kelp. Far away fisherman in bobbing boats looked delicate as water spiders, mysterious as ghosts.

Looking back toward shore everything seemed insignificant—buildings and airplanes, crowds busy doing nothing. Out at sea, our smallness was wonderful. We were no more important than floating seaweed or a floating plastic bag.

Here I found peace, acceptance and courage, to realize all I didn't know. All I wanted was to experience the buoyancy of water, feel weightless, timeless, full.

Eventually our limbs grew tired so we braved it back to shore, through waves that tossed us and pummeled us clean. When our toes touched bottom, we waded ashore stupefied and purified and completely renewed.

My earliest memories of State Beach are of riding in the back seat of our pale green, 1953 Chevy convertible. From Overland Avenue we passed the Olympic drive-in on the corner of Bundy, with its huge mural of a woman in a two-piece bathing suit, riding a long wooden surf board. I wonder if my mother ever missed teaching Sunday school, or worshiping with her friends at church? Often she'd suggest that we take a drive up the coast—maybe all the way to Santa Barbara, but I don't remember it ever happening. Instead almost every weekend she packed us up and off we headed.

In those days the beach was full of seaweed. I was allowed to suck on the delicious salty bulbs. New ones were thick and juicy. I'd bite off the tip and suck out the delicious viscous liquid. Old ones were dry as jerky, with crisp, fish-like tails. Yum, my salty pacifier.

State Beach was narrower than it is today. The "polio pond" marked the northern border. The sun-warmed lagoon formed from creek water was a perfect place for us kids to play. We loved wading in the shallow tepid water. A small spit of sand formed an island where we could build sand castles without fear of them being swept to sea. In those days we didn't think about getting sick from playing in the stagnant water. In winter rains flushed it out, and our trickling creek turned into a roaring river that deposited trees and all sorts of rubbish all over along the shore.

Just south of the polio pond, a Spanish-style stucco building, that had originally been a concession stand, housed the Santa Monica lifeguard headquarters and dim public restrooms. I didn't like the feel of the cold, wet, gritty cement floor. Outside the restroom was a cold-water shower. What a relief, to hold open the front of my rubbery, red, one-piece bathing suit and let fresh cold water rush over me, making me gasp. How good it felt to get rid of all that clingy, itchy sand.

Next to the restrooms a flight of stairs connected to the parking lot. Half-way up was a ledge where boys yelled like Tarzan and jumped off into the sand near the chess players and volleyball players who sat against the wall.

Down closer to the ocean artists and writers sat, the people my mother preferred. To her they were more interesting. My mom and dad would join this group, set up their green canvas back rests, spread out their towels, and settle in. In a little while my father would wander back up to the wall toward the lifeguard station where he mixed with the Hollywood crowd. I remember him being surrounded by people, right in the midst of everything. I could always find him in a crowd because his tan, muscular, six-foot-three frame towered over everyone around him.

Early in their marriage, my father introduced my mother to Jo Lathwood, niece of artist Mary Cassatt. Jo was fifteen years older than my mother, but they became best friends. Jo had been a Las Vegas dancer and was now a water color artist and sports wear designer. She designed the first two-piece "wrap around" bathing suits in the 1950s and the first bikinis in the early 1960s.

Jo lived with Ben Massalink, who we called Benjie, a writer. He was my mother's age. Their little one-bedroom apartment, a block from State Beach, had grass matting on the floors and bright-colored walls decorated with paintings from the many famous artists they knew. Jo and Benjie spent every winter in a tropical climate, where Jo painted and Benjie wrote, and they lived in grass shacks or cheap hotels. I was closer to Jo and Benjie than to my working-class uncles and their families who lived "way over" in Glendale.

Twice I remember my family getting dressed up to greet Jo and Benjie after one of their three-month trips. The first time I was six. Mother put all of us in 1920s clothes (remember, this was the 1950s and so flapper clothes were still easy to find in thrift shops). In the photo my dad is wearing a "morning coat" and top hat, but on his feet he has on his usual white *zories*. Mother, Ann and I are in chiffon dresses and cloche hats. Mother said we were pretending to be missionaries.

The second time I was thirteen. Mother thought it would be funny to disguise ourselves as cameras. So my father painted three big cardboard boxes black, tacked on two pie tins to look like lenses and made plaques that said Gowlandflex for the tops. He made a smaller version for my baby niece Tracy, who was not yet a year old, that said Rolleiflex on top. We ran down the corridor of the airport dragging the boxes. Ann placed Tracy's car seat on the floor and hid her behind it. The three of us got into our boxes. Of course these were the days long before metal detectors, when you could go directly to the gangway to meet your friends. Travelers and their friends gathered around to see was going on. We couldn't see Jo and Benjie's reaction, of course because we were hidden, but when we came out Jo clapped her hands and Benjie just shook his head, laughing. Airport workers were so nice, they disposed of the boxes for us.

In the early photos of my mother at the beach her skin is milk white. But over the years she became as brown as her friends. I can still my see the lines of wood-framed back rests, the rows of white *zories,* the bright green swim fins with a hole over the arch of the foot. Everyone wore sunglasses and slathered themselves with Sea & Ski, or Coppertone, and in the 1960s waxy orange Bain du Soliel. Some wore straw hats. I loved the white plastic eye protectors that looked like egg shells. How funny it was to see white eyelids and crow's feet on an otherwise nut-brown face. We didn't think about skin cancer then.

South of my parents group, just before The Beach Club, with its pretty blue and white awnings and tidy rows of navy blue umbrellas set up down by the water, was the gay beach: slender young men with smooth slim bodies in tiny black Speedos. I liked to watch them toss Frisbees or jog. They were all so gorgeous.

One day when I was seven, I was playing in the churning surf. I caught a wave and rode it to shore. Just as I was about to stand up, a toddler fell right on top of me. I couldn't get up. My face was underwater. I thought, *I'm going to drown."* It couldn't have been more than a few seconds, but it felt like ages. I held my breath as long as I could, until finally the mother pulled the child off of me.

I got up onto my hands and knees spitting sand, coughing. My ears rang. Before the next wave could gobble me up, I hobbled up the beach to find my mother. The tide had carried me far down the beach. I made my way up to Mother, reclining elegantly against her backrest. I flopped down next to her and let out a huge sigh.

She put her arms around me and laughed. "You looked like a drowned rat! And you're caked with sand. Go shower off honey, it'll make you feel better."

I trudged across the hot sand toward the outdoor shower. I could see my father among his harem of starlets. Suddenly my foot was on fire. I had stepped on a burning cigarette! I ran the rest of the way crying. My father held the shower on for me, as my salty tears mixed with the salty sea water. My father picked me up and carried me back to my towel where I sat glumly the rest of the day, watching a red welt form on the bottom of my foot.

Worse than the pain was the realization that there was danger in the world, I really could have drowned. I could get hurt. Things didn't seem so safe anymore.

IN THE LIFEGUARD'S ARMS

I was born by the ocean
it is not a metaphor
my powerful, seemingly placid
neighbor.

Foamy waves gurgled around me
then my face was in the sand
I was pinned underwater by
a toddler who'd fallen
on top of me.
I couldn't breathe.

I imagined my thin girl body
carried to my mother
who would be
too stunned to cry
seeing her small limp daughter
in the lifeguard's arms.

But I sat up
sputtered, stumbled
to the outdoor shower.
I stepped on a cigarette.
My foot got burned.

I shivered in the rush
of cold chlorinated water
as it rinsed my salty terror
and gave me
an exhilarated glow
an eagerness to grow
into womanhood
where I would never again
feel like a drowning child.

When I was eight, my parents and their friends prepared for a long swim south to the jetty. I can see them now, walking down to the water, carrying their fins. My mother in a blue-and-white, Hawaiian print two-piece, pauses to tuck her short blonde hair into a white bathing cap and snaps the strap under her chin. She bends one leg and puts on her fin, then the other, and waddles the rest of the way into the waves.

I wanted so badly to join them. So on this particular day I decided it wasn't too far. I was a good swimmer. My father taught me in our swimming pool, holding on to my bathing suit straps until I could swim all by myself.

I waited until everyone had gone out beyond the waves and then I ran after them. It took me a long time to get past the waves. You're supposed to count, and after the seventh wave, there should be a lull. But I lost count and decided to just brave it. I took a deep breath as the next wave came crashing toward me, closed my eyes, dove straight under it, kicked with all my might, then shot up out of the water. I'd made it!

I was out where it was calm and sea gulls bobbed. I rested a while, floating on my back, catching my breath. I could see my parents and their friends far south of me their heads getting smaller and smaller, heading toward the pier. I started after them, swimming dog-paddle, the only way I knew.

"Wait for me!" I cried but no one heard. I started to get tired. What had I done? They didn't know I was out here. What if I couldn't catch up and I got carried out to sea? Finally my mother's white head stopped and turned. She heard me! I waved. She waved back. I kept swimming. She treaded water, waiting for me to catch up. I was so proud of myself, but sorry I had made her stop her graceful overhand strokes and wait for me. Everyone continued on. I caught up with my mother and even though she scolded me, I could tell she was proud of me. She told me when to start kicking and we rode a wave to shore. While everyone else jogged on ahead, my mother and I walked together. I liked having her all to myself.

By the time I was twelve, my friends and I were allowed to walk to the beach and spend all day next to lifeguard tower number four. There were two ways to get there. We could climb the ivy-covered fence in the Spivak's yard into Rustic Canyon Park, then walk down Latimer Road, past Lee Marvin's house and down Mesa Road. There we could continue on Mesa to Channel Road or take a set of steep stairs down to West Channel. Then take the stinky underpass.

Or we could take a more direct route, the creek—which I wrote about in chapter three—and come out in the Polio Pond. Some times of year tides were so strong they created mini-palisades along the shore.

CLIFFS

formed by winter waves
that scoop like
mechanical earthmover claws
taking chunk after chunk
back to sea
we love to
run up to the brink
hold our breaths
then slide down
to the hard wet sand.

Up and down we fall
explorers finding out a lot about

ourselves, at twelve
breasts
begin to ache
the beginning of ache
the beginning of longing
the summer of moo moos
and menstruation
wanting, not wanting
to be seen
wanting to be invisible
yet beautiful.

Silly, pointed, skinny
so thin and frail
who will take you seriously?
and blonde besides
with a father besides
who flirts with women on the beach
women with round breasts
and smooth torsos
in strapless bikinis.

In 1961 it is very daring
to walk around and lie around
with cleavage and a navel
exposed to men's eyes.

At twelve I know what men want.

If only time would hurry up
and change the shape of me
the way waves carve the beach

the way being touched
transfuses what might
have died.

In the early 1960s my father bought a Lambretta motor scooter. He could now zip down to the beach and not have sit in traffic or pay for parking. On my twelfth birthday I had a pool party. As a special treat my father gave each of my friends a ride down to the beach and back. It was only a mile, after all, so each trip was about ten minutes. Sometimes I loved having a cool dad. I can see him in his red swim trunks, no shirt, rubber thongs, curly brown hair, brown skin, blue eyes, sitting so straight on his scooter with one of my friends on back, holding him around the waist.

More and more he'd go to the beach alone and Mother could do the Sunday Times crossword or spend time with me and my friends. She'd sit with me and Susie and Teresa at the dining room table and draw, play Life or canasta. She'd play the piano and we'd practice songs for an upcoming party, such as *Shanty in Old Shanty Town* or *Cry Me a River*.

When we heard the putt-putt of the scooter, we'd say, "He's home!" and put away what we were doing.

Sometimes he'd stay so late, dinner would almost be ready when Mother called the phone at State Beach. Anyone who answered would know my father and find him, or give him the message.

For teenagers, going to the beach was more than socializing and swimming. We were there to get tan. After our long day at the beach, my friends and I loved to compare tan lines. Our goal was to look like we were wearing a white bathing suit when we were naked. The most serious tanners brought folding reflectors and held them under their baby-oiled faces, basically frying to a crisp. We combed hydrogen peroxide through our hair. By the end of summer it was the color of straw.

When I was little, lunch meant accompanying my parents to Ted's Grill where we sat in red vinyl booths and ordered steak sandwiches on grilled sourdough, clam chowder and fresh blueberry cobbler. As teens we ran across the highway (now there are barriers) and ate hamburgers in little wooden booths at Roy's Diner next to the Chevron station. Then we'd go to Canyon Liquor for a strawberry yogurt, Orange Crush and Cheetos.

In Home Economics class I made my first bikini, taking apart one of Jo Lathwood's suits to use as a pattern. I bought bright yellow cotton and white eyelet ruffle, one row for the bra and three for the back of the bottom. It was adorable, one-of-a-kind, and gave a little shape to my skinny thirteen-year-old figure.

One day sunbathing with my girlfriends, a group of boys surrounded us. They were the popular jocks, most a year or two older. I felt flattered. For a moment I felt like one of the models my father photographed, and basked in the attention. Then suddenly they stood up, all at once. They grabbed me by the wrists and ankles and roughly carried me into the surf. They dumped me, laughing, jumping against the waves. I was humiliated and confused but part of me loved the attention. This became a routine, just part of a day at the beach. When they started to gather around, I'd try to relax, and when I felt their hands on me I'd go limp, take a big breath and wait for it to be over.

I guess I took the fun out of it when I stopped fighting and squealing for them to stop, because one day they lingered a little longer than usual, lying on their stomachs, fiddling with pieces of polished glass. Then they all stood up at once. Their silhouettes threw me into shadow. I squinted up at the circle of young males surrounding me with their beach-y hormonal smell.

In an instant, one of them ripped off my bra and waved it like a flag. My friend Kathie jumped up and started pummeling him with her fists. She grabbed my top and he took off running. The rest of the boys followed, running into the ocean, attacking the waves as they whooped and hollered.

Kathie wrapped her towel around me and sat with me until I stopped shaking. I didn't go back to State Beach the rest of that summer. I went further up the coast, to Neeny's instead, with Susie and Teresa and their friends from Corpus Christi School. State Beach wasn't safe anymore.

Chapter 11

GOD & GRANDMOTHERS

I knew my mom had been a Sunday school teacher before she met my father. I wonder if she ever asked him to go to church with her. If she did he said no. As a little boy, when his dad was working on a movie out of town, Peter stayed at Baby Land whose owners were Christian Scientist. He came away with the belief that the body heals itself and always avoided going to doctors. But he never talked about spiritual or religious matters. He had a strong affinity for animals, particularly wildlife. I had the impression he respected them more than he did humans. When one of my cats killed a mother bird he gave the cat away. And in his later years he spent thousands of dollars on bags of dry dog food feeding the wild raccoons, possums, even coyotes who showed up every night at dusk. As for Sundays, as I've said, State Beach took the place of church in our lives.

So, where did I get my ideas about God? My father recorded these two quotes from me, when I was four:

> Mary Lee said at breakfast "You know what I dreamed last night? I went up to see God. You know what I said? 'God you're pretty. God I like you. God you smell good.'" And then she started singing a little song she made up about God in heaven, help me to buy a doll.

> Another time Mary Lee had been thinking about God and she came into the office where Alice was typing. "Mommy you know up in heaven there's a big purple octopus and he has strings tied to his arms . . . and you know what? We're puppets."

I have a vague memory of going to a dark, brick, Presbyterian Sunday School, near Grandma's house (my mother's mother) when I was little, learning about David and Goliath, and singing "Jesus Loves Me."

Grandma had pure white hair, worn up in a conservative bun. She always wore dark, shapeless dresses, stockings, sensible black shoes and pearls. She lived in a tiny, meticulous duplex in the old part of Los Angeles, on a hilly street near Currie's Ice Cream parlor, within walking distance of Safeway Market. She lived an orderly life that she recorded in her Daily Reminder: Sunday—church; Monday—laundry; Tuesday—ironing; Wednesday—canasta with lady friends; Thursday—grocery shopping; Friday—housecleaning; Saturday—visits with her grandchildren. Sunday—church.

Grandma was very close to her sons Ted and Don. Uncle Ted didn't have children until his third marriage, but Uncle Don had five kids, so Grandma got to spend time with them. Because we lived a good forty-five minutes away, we saw her less often. In fact, I remember screaming fights with Mother, begging her not to make me spend the night at Grandma's. I didn't want to be separated from my cats, my home, my friends.

Once I got there, though, it wasn't so bad. I liked the fragrant hard, oval bars of Sweetheart soap, her claw-foot bathtub. I liked sleeping in the same room as Grandma, in twin beds separated by a narrow nightstand. She put her teeth in a glass of water before bed, and snored softly in her sleep.

Grandma's tiny front room contained a small sofa and two wing-back chairs, one upholstered in light blue brocade, the other in a navy blue fabric similar to corduroy with wide whales that I loved to run my fingernails over. The chairs and couch had claw feet and arms, so I had the wonderful feeling of sitting in a huge nest. Built-in cabinets with glass doors contained her collection of porcelain figurines.

When my mother, Don and Ted were little, their parents bought them a ten-volume, gold leaf, *The Bible and Its Story* with wonderful black lithograph illustrations. Mother and her brothers liked to leaf through it, looking for pictures of naked women. I can tell where the binding is worn which pictures they looked at most: Eve being expelled from the Garden, "The Comfort of Eve" naked, cradling Cain and Abel, etc.

Grandma was only eight-years older than Andy, my father's mother, but seemed more conservative and traditional. Andy had left England to pursue her dream of being an actress, married my grandfather, divorced, remarried, divorced again. In her fifties she had a crush on a man she called Swami who my parents thought was a charlatan.

When I was born Andy passed down to me a little leather-bound boxed set, *Common Prayer* and *Holy Bible*. The print is so small I can hardly read it. On the front page of the Bible inscribed in pencil it says, *Mary B. Harvey July 1848*. She was Andy's grandmother. Beneath this in black ink, *B.S. Bird, 60 DeBeauvoir St, London N.E.* That's Andy. Her birth name was Beatrice Sylvia Bird. Below that in blue ink, *Mary Lee Gowland, May 6th-'49 California*.

I also have Andy's 1935 edition of *The Prophet* by Kahlil Gibran, *The Autobiography of Gandhi* and *The Autobiography of a Yogi* by Paramahansa Yogananda, who came to America in 1920 to teach meditation. He founded the Self Realization Fellowship in Encinitas, California. I attended Sunday services in the 1980s at the Self Realization Fellowship Lake Shrine in Pacific Palisades, and took their correspondence course in Kriya Yoga.

I always felt close to Andy. She had big hazel eyes and a kind smile. When she came to Hollywood she sold her knee-length hair to Max Factor, make-up artist and wig maker, who became a cosmetics manufacturer.

Andy's health was delicate. My father said she once drove across the country and was so poor she made tea with radiator water and it made her sick. The "miscarriage" she had before my father was conceived was actually a self-administered abortion. She nearly died from peritonitis. The intestinal blockage that killed her at the age of sixty-three might have been caused by scar tissue from that horrible procedure.

Plus, Andy suffered from schizophrenia. In her forties and fifties she had run-ins with the law. She was arrested for hosing down a passerby outside her Hollywood apartment. A psychiatrist determined that she should receive shock treatments, so she was sent to the state mental hospital in Camarillo.

I remember visiting her but not being allowed to go inside because I was too young. I sat on the wide green lawns under willowy eucalyptus trees and stared up at the barred windows.

Andy's acting career consisted of small "bit parts." One was a mental patient in the 1948 movie *The Snake Pit*, starring Olivia de Havilland. VideoHound calls it "One of the first films to compassionately explore mental illness and its treatment." The photograph my father took of Andy, for the casting call, shows a middle aged woman with a tormented expression glaring into the camera.

But I never saw the dark side of Andy. To me she was more like a fairy godmother with her English accent who lived in an silver Airstream in a Santa Monica Trailer-Park. I loved to sit across from her at the little table and drink tea from delicate china cups. In one corner she had a shelf of small miniature brass objects including a Chinese gong that became one of my favorite toys.

My neighbor Susie made me realize that not everyone had the same idea of God as I did. Shortly after we moved in to our new house, she and I were standing in my parents' office. The cork-board walls displayed 14"x20" black and white prints. Some were nudes.

Susie studied one of the nudes a long time and then said authoritatively, "You probably won't go to hell, but your father will."

How did she know this? I soon found out. One Sunday I went to church with Pat and the girls and experienced my first Catholic Mass. I loved the church's high ceilings and stained glass windows. The incense smelled delicious. I liked the glowing candles and shimmering brocade vestments. The life-size statues of Mary and Jesus and various saints were very realistic. I liked how parishioners anointed themselves with holy water from a font and genuflected before they took their seats in the pews. I loved the sound of Latin, the ringing of bells and solemn music from a big pipe organ.

I learned from Susie about confession, how you could do just about anything and be forgiven if you just said some *Hail Marys* and *Our Fathers*. I wanted to hold a black rosary and intone prayers over and over, as I fingered the smooth beads. But of course, I wasn't Catholic. I could only observe.

The best part of being a Catholic girl was the possibility that one day you could become the bride of Christ. This was even better than marrying a prince. And nuns did good works, such as hiding Jewish children from Nazis, or administering to lepers in Africa. *The Nun's Story*, from 1959, starring Audrey Hepburn, was one of our favorite movies. And remember, Susie promised herself to God when she was twelve. Just being around her made me feel closer to the Heavenly Father.

Every night before I fell asleep I prayed, "Now I lay me down to sleep, I pray the Lord my soul to keep, If I should die before I wake, I pray the Lord, my soul to take. God Bless everyone in the world, amen. Good night Sweet Lord. Amen." I was confident God looked out for me. I loved Jesus but I wanted a real, live, flesh-and-blood male to love.

Finally, at age fourteen, I found one at the Bay Theater, just down the street from Corpus Christi Church.

Chapter 12

THE BAY THEATER

The Bay Theater, on Sunset Boulevard in Pacific Palisades, was built in 1948 and remained a single-screen theater until the early 1970s. For a brief time it became a twin-screen theater, but sadly it closed in 1978 and in 1980 Norris Hardware moved in.

Across the street were The Hot Dog Show, a tiny hot dog and hamburger joint that looked like a doll house; Palisades Stationers, where I loved to get lost in the delicious smells of leather portfolios, wooden pencils and crisp typing paper; House of Lee, the Chinese restaurant where I developed my love of Chinese food, and where Mother came up with so many of our Christmas card ideas.

In junior high, my girlfriends and I liked to hang out at the Bay Pharmacy, next door to the Bay Theater. One counter lady had huge, stiff, ratted, gray hair and extremely long painted fingernails. We spent hours testing lipsticks and spritzing each other with Jean Nate, Shalimar, Maja and other colognes. We all hated Jungle Gardenia. When I was fourteen, I bought two flavored lipsticks—caramel and pink peppermint that I hoped one day a boyfriend would kiss off.

Orange and green terrazzo linked the pharmacy with the entrance to the movie theater. When my parents built their house, they chose terrazzo too—white with grey and black specks—because they said it was so practical, you could just hose it down after a party, although they never really did this. In 1959, when my sister Ann was sixteen, her friend, as an initiation into the Premiers, their YWCA sponsored service club, had to scrub the terrazzo with a toothbrush one Saturday night.

The lobby of the theater had dark red carpet and smelled of fresh popcorn and real melted butter. The concession stand where we bought our Milk Duds and Slo-Poke suckers, was on the left next to a wide stairway leading up to the balcony and rest rooms.

How many hundreds of movies did we see there? New movies came out on Wednesdays. As little kids we loved to spend half a Saturday at a matinee: cartoon, newsreel, coming attractions and *two* movies. My friends got upset with me when I told them the lava in *The Seventh Voyage of Sinbad* was actually oatmeal with a red light on it. My dad had taught me well.

In junior high, the Bay Theater was *the* place to be on Friday nights. Our parents dropped us off and picked us up after the double-feature which meant we had three or four hours with our friends, unsupervised.

On the right side of the theater girls sat with girlfriends hoping boys they liked would sit behind them, maybe kick their seat. The boys knew who we liked: we wrote their names in big dark letters on our denim three-ring binders. I had crushes on John Tuttle, Johnny Shea, and Pete Colby but they never acknowledged me.

Couples paired off on the left side of the theater. A boy would start by holding his girl's hand or put his arm on the back of her chair, then let it gently slip down and rest on her shoulder—but not her breast! Discreet kissing would ensue, with the arm rest between them.

I remember a girl who had no friends. She would arrived alone, sit by herself until a guy sat down beside her, then together they'd sneak out into the alley. I used to imagine what it was like to be her.

THE LOOK

What was it like to stand
against the stucco wall of the Bay Theater
with the corner streetlight casting
shadows on her and whichever boy
she had chosen that night?

We could imagine metal braces
cutting into swollen lips, because
we had braces too and we allowed
boys to kiss us
during Doris Day movies.

But we didn't know what it was like
to sneak outside and let guys
in white socks and black loafers
feel us up.

We didn't know how she felt
with her mouth on the back
of their sunburned necks
while they gave her
a bright red hickey
that would mark her all week
as a slut because
we pushed our boyfriends away
even though we wanted
to feel what was buttoned
inside their jeans.

Weren't we eager to unclasp
our bras and free ourselves
and find our sexuality
and find we were a gift?

What we didn't see was
the look they gave her
not after, but during,
a look of such profound gratitude
a look that was all she needed
to endure the rest of the week,
the same look we would see
years later in the eyes of men
who made us feel like angels
with the power to give so much
by just being ourselves.

Mr. Szabo, the theater manager had a thick Eastern European accent. Before each show he stood in front of the screen in his military-style uniform, and gave us the same old lecture on how to behave, which invariably elicited smirks and cat calls. During the show he'd patrol the aisles with his flashlight, and shine it in the face of anyone who had their feet on the seat in front of them. I don't ever remember adults in the theater on Friday nights. If they were there, they probably sat up in the balcony.

November 22, 1963 fell on a Friday. I was talking to a friend outside the Student Store, discussing our upcoming A9-B9 football game. She and I were two of six cheerleaders of the A9 team—the summer graduating class. Our mothers had made our darling uniforms: short, yellow-and-white gingham skirts with suspenders, over white blouses with Peter Pan collars. We planned to practice after school. One of our new cheers went "Pork chops, pork chops, greasy, greasy, we're going to win this easy, easy."

Suddenly we heard someone yell "Kennedy's been shot!" Anxiety swept through the crowd. How could we find out if he was okay? Then a moment later the Principal's voice came over the PA system. All after school activities were canceled. He said to proceed immediately to our next classes and our teachers would fill us in. The whole school became quiet as we walked, in a daze, to our different rooms.

Our teacher told us someone had shot President Kennedy. He was in a hospital in Dallas, Texas. "Let's have a moment of silence and pray for him," she said. We bowed our heads.

We all knew that President Lincoln had been assassinated at the Ford Theater and that Garfield and McKinley had also be killed in office. Now we too were part of history! I still didn't believe Kennedy would die. He was so charismatic. Almost everyone I knew loved him. Back in sixth grade, at Canyon Elementary School, my friends and I linked arms and paraded around the playground singing his campaign song, "High Hopes."

By the time I got home President Kennedy was dead. I found my parents sitting on the couch staring at the black-and-white TV. They had both been crying. Even Walter Cronkite looked like he was crying!

Suddenly I felt furious. How could one evil person ruin everything? What would happen next? That awful Johnson would be president. And poor Jackie with two little kids! I couldn't stand to think about it. I had to get out of the house. Thank God I had the Bay Theater to escape to.

I called Heidi, my friend since Kindergarten. She said her family was going to temple. Great. Well, I wasn't about to sit home and cry. I couldn't stand to keep watching Jackie's tear-streaked face, and the usually stalwart Chet Huntley and David Brinkley visibly shaken.

I'd actually seen JFK a few months before. He and a bunch of people were walking on the beach in front of his brother-in-law, Peter Lawford's house, a few doors south of State Beach. And now he was dead? I couldn't stand to think about it.

So Mother dropped me off at the Bay Theater.

I couldn't really concentrate on *The Wheeler Dealers* starring James Garner. The theater was barely half-full and no one messed around. We all just stared at the screen in stunned silence until the lights came up. Then we quietly filed out into the cool fall air, and waited for our parents to take us home.

The pall hung over us through the next week. The A9-B9 football game was played with little excitement. It was as if we all had the flu and just wanted to go to bed. Lyndon Johnson became President and no one I knew was happy about it.

On December 31, 1963 Heidi had a slumber party. Her gregarious mom, Sylvia, who loved to sit in Heidi's lavender room and gossip with us, would be out with her dad. Grandma Esther would be "in charge."

Because we were on Christmas vacation, it wasn't as easy to spread the word about the party, but we still hoped that boys would crash it, and so we dressed accordingly in our prettiest, sexiest nightgowns—as opposed to how we dressed for a Kidnap Breakfast when we went out to Uncle John's Pancake House and had to be modest.

I chose between two negligees I'd borrowed from the models' dressing room. The navy blue slip Mother pinned to fit, when I was five and pretended to be sing "Auld Lang Syne" for our 1954 Christmas card now fit. But I chose a pink negligee with a sweeping floor-length skirt and black brocade bodice that made me feel like Loretta Young. I could wear a bra with it, and the black satin ribbon, that tied in the back, made my waist look small.

In the drawer of a speaker cabinet my dad had made years ago, a little vial of Tabu perfume had been forgotten. Mother said it had been a gift to her when I was born. I don't remember her ever wearing any perfume, which is why it was probably forgotten in that drawer. I loved to open that little bottle and take a whiff. It had an exotic spicy smell. Getting ready for the party, I dabbed Tabu behind my ears and was transported to a Middle Eastern harem.

I remember Heidi's kitchen so clearly—the little table by the sunny window, the clock on the wall. But I don't remember what we ate for dinner. Grandma Esther retired to the den to watch TV and we had the elegant living room—the room that was only used on special occasions—all to ourselves.

Sure enough, in a little while the doorbell rang. Giddy with excitement Heidi opened the door to a cluster of boys on the porch.

They tromped in and joined us in that immaculate Asian-inspired room. Heidi put on *Meet the Beatles* and soon we were dancing to "She Love You," then Rolling Stones' and Beach Boys' songs.

Kathie snuck off down the hall with her boyfriend Tom, to make out in Heidi's bedroom. Other couples paired off and I found myself with a stocky varsity football player I'd never even spoken to. I liked the smell and feel of his leather letterman jacket when we wedged between the piano and the living room wall. I loved feeling his muscular body pressing into me. I was finally making out! Breathlessly I relaxed against him and received my first hickey. I surrendered to his strong, tender embrace thinking how different from clutching my pillow, or my cat.

At some point Grandma Ester came out of the den, found the boys and kicked them out. We retreated to Heidi's bedroom to gossip and compare hickeys. I remember the fluorescent bathroom light and how my friends were so surprised and proud of me.

I had gotten my period at twelve, but now I really felt I'd become a woman.

By the time school started my hickey had faded to lavender and yellow. I wore a turtleneck to hide it from my parents and my teachers, and checked it several times a day in the girls' bathroom. The football player didn't call me. But I didn't really care. I had been initiated and was now ready for my true love to come into my life.

On Friday, January 14, 1964 *Lawrence of Arabia* debuted at the Bay Theater. I wanted to sit right smack-dab in the middle of the theater because it had been filmed in Cinemascope, which meant extra-wide. The theater was almost full. I found my friends and sat down. Just as the lights went down, Lenny, the sixteen-year-old brother of one of my classmates took the seat next to me. I briefly acknowledged him, but was engrossed in the booming music and the mesmerizing image of Peter O'Toole riding a camel through an undulating desert.

But then, as the movie got underway, something weird happened. The boy beside me seemed to be emitting electricity that reached over the arm of the chair and made my arm tingle. I was embarrassed and didn't want to look at him, but finally I needed to see if he felt it too. I turned my head and our eyes met. The electricity entered my eyes, traveled down my neck, swirled around my breasts, and coursed through my blood until I felt my whole body purring.

My eyes shot back to the screen, but the invisible barrier that had caused me to feel like a separate individual my entire life had dissolved. I put my hand on the armrest between us. He took my hand. We sat like that the entire movie—three and a half hours—and when the lights came up at the end, I knew my life had changed forever.

The next day, Saturday, Lenny called. We talked on the phone five hours, setting the phone down only when we had to pee or get something to eat. Neither of us wanted to hang up, but our ears ached and our mothers were calling us for dinner.

Sunday it rained. Lenny came and picked me up in his mother's huge Ford Fairlane station wagon, and drove us down to State Beach, where we parked and made out for hours. The windows steamed. Lenny was short. We could completely lie down together in the back seat.

My first letter from him reads:

> Honey, Sweetheart, Darling Mary Lee . . . how the heck are you? (only wonderful) I'm doing my homework now, its night and I should be kissing you instead but you know how it is. I didn't wash my hands because I like the smell of the perfume you wear, or whatever it is. Your hair smells good too. (You must think I'm crazy) but I'm not really. Well, however you look at it I think you're great, regardless of what I say or act like. AND I do love you so much, and hope it works the other way. Well I have to work out some incomplete quadratic equations for geometry so I'll say good-bye for now. Be sure to write me and give it to my sister but seal it so she doesn't read the priceless words.
>
> I love you . . .

Lenny asked me to go steady and presented me with an oval St. Christopher medal on a gold chain. He was Jewish and I was Protestant but this was the tradition. Of course I said yes. I never took it off.

One weekend, when my parents were gone—probably down at the beach taking pictures—Kathie and Lenny's sister, Arlene, came over. We decided to dress up and take pictures in the studio. We had so much fun. I put a roll of 2 ¼" film into one of my dad's Hasselblads and screwed it into the rolling camera stand.

We rummaged around in the models' dressing room and found various costumes.

Arlene looked alluring clutching a white fox stole around her shoulders. Kathie put on a top hat, long white gloves and held a sign that read "I'm Miss Kleenex 1965." Arlene found some fake grapes and lay holding them over her mouth like a Roman goddess.

I'd recently bought a push-up bra and wore it under a pretty lacy slip. My breasts were still small, so I used one of the tricks I knew about modeling. I clutched my arms around my chest and leaned forward, creating a pretty decent cleavage. This would be the picture I'd give Lenny, to carry in his wallet. He'd like the shadow his Saint Christopher medal cast on my chest, and my pouty lips.

Suddenly we heard a knock on the *soji*-screen door. "What are you girls up to?" came the booming voice of George, one of my dad's employees, a big man with rough hands. He slid the door open and stood in his machinist's apron glaring at us.

"Nothing!" I answered, getting up from the floor. "We're just taking pictures." I slid the door closed in his face. Kathie, behind the camera stand, gave me a wide-eyed stare and put her hand over her mouth. Arlene poked her head out of the dressing room.

"Don't you do anything nasty now!" George said behind the screen.

"We're not!" I yelled back. I looked at my friends and we stifled our giggles until we heard George go back out into the garage, then we burst out laughing.

We took three rolls of pictures. For the first time in my life I was posing for someone other than my father. I had a real, live boy who loved me. Nothing could be better.

That June I wore Lenny's Saint Christopher with the beautiful pink and white silk dress Mother made me, to our ninth grade Grad Night. Lenny and I double dated with another couple. My dad took pictures of the boys pinning white orchids on our dresses.

1964 was the happiest year of my life, so far. I spent most of the summer on Topanga Beach, a few miles up from State Beach, at Lenny's family's little beach house. I loved watching Lenny and his friends surf. His mom was so cool. She never minded feeding all the hungry, sandy kids who never wanted to go home.

Lenny's best friend was the son of one of the writers of *I Love Lucy*, and other shows. Tom was a crack up, with a wry self-effacing sense of humor. He always had a twinkle in his eye. He went on to be one of the original writers on Saturday Night Live and has had a successful career as a director. That summer, he and I spent hours lying on the sand, side by side, talking and laughing. Lenny was never jealous. He knew I was in love with him. We were soul mates. No one would ever come between us.

William, another of Lenny's friends, was the son of a famous movie director. He was an agile surfer who liked to take risks and could stay on a board in the roughest surf. I loved when the guys walked out of the surf, after hours riding waves. Dripping wet and exhausted from hours out in the ocean, they carried their long surfboards under their arms and dropped them on the sand with a *thunk,* then plopped themselves down on a towel. Their diaphragms rose and fell until their breathing slowed. Their faces had the look of complete contentment.

I was so happy when school started in the fall because Lenny and I could finally be together during the school day. He was a senior and I was a sophomore at Pali Hi (Palisades High School). I asked him for his class schedule so I could "run into him" during breaks, even if I had to run half-way across campus to do so. We would meet up at Nutrition (morning break) and lunch. After school he could take me home. I was in heaven.

Lenny's family lived within walking distance of the Riviera Country Club which offered an after-school dance class. Kathie, Arlene and I signed up. Our teacher taught us The Swim, The

Bugaloo, The Frug and The Jerk. We then would teach them to our other friends, at Friday night dances at the local Y. Most boys just kind of wiggled around in time to the music. Some liked to see how lewd they could be before a chaperone tapped them on the shoulder and told them to behave.

After our weekly after-school dance class, we'd go back to Kathie's or Arlene's for a snack and to just hang out. More and more I wanted to go to Arlene's so I could see Lenny. Staying for dinner evolved into dinner and spending the night.

Lenny and I devised a routine: after dinner Arlene and I would get ready for bed. I would have brought one of the models' negligees, no cotton PJs for me! Once Arlene was asleep I'd tiptoe past their two German shepherds sleeping outside their parents' bedroom, and into Lenny and his little brother's room.

It's a good thing his brother was a deep sleeper, because Lenny and I would cuddle all night in his narrow twin bed. I'd slip off my nightie and lie in his arms, wearing only underpants, which prevented us from actually going "all the way." Just before dawn I'd reluctantly tiptoe back past his parents' bedroom, give the dogs a scratch behind their ears, and slip into bed in Arlene's room.

In January 1965 I got my braces off. Four years of torture were finally over. For one whole year I'd been kissing Lenny with those awful metal bands on my teeth. My poor mouth had been through so much. With my braces gone, my teeth were smooth and slippery. I could eat anything I wanted and kissing Lenny became even more wonderful than before.

On Saturday nights after Lenny and I had gone to a movie, or a party, we liked to park on Latimer Road before he took me home.

LATIMER ROAD

When we first parked on Latimer Road
in your mother's Ford Fairlane station wagon,
I knew I had found my life.
My small girl body in your small boy arms
I lay stretched out on the long seat,

all five-feet-four of me beside
all five-feet-five or you,
your sixteen-year-old lips
on my fifteen-year-old lips
the night like sulfur, luminous
with crickets and the
wet marshy smell of the creek
and the wet musky smell of us
like late summer plums
the clean cotton of your ironed shirt
twill pants, white socks,
my ribbed top, hip huggers and
sandals showing off my painted toes.
You kissed my toes, remember?
You kissed every inch of me in that
gigantic automobile that was
large enough to contain
the anxious bud of adolescence
before it became too ripe, before
it soured, before I wept in bed
unable to eat because you had
vanished from my life
gone off to college
where girls were not girls anymore
where you were no longer a boy
where you became many things
not one of which was mine.

I wrote that poem in 1996 as a way to neatly tie up the incapacitating heartache I experienced when Lenny broke up with me. But what really happened was this: Lenny and I thought I was pregnant.

My period was late. All those nights cuddling in his narrow bed, I had kept my panties on, so he never actually entered me. But was it possible that semen could swim up my leg, through my underpants and get inside me, without me knowing? It was awfully wet down there.

I told Lenny over the phone. I was too afraid to see his face. He was quiet for a minute then he said, "I'll call you back."

I waited an hour, sitting on my bed, petting my black cat, trying to be comforted by his purring. When the phone rang I nearly jumped off the bed.

"You have to pee in a jar," Lenny said. "Put the jar in a brown paper bag and leave it in your locker. I'll take it to a clinic."

I gave him my locker combination. "How long will it take to find out?"

"A few days," he said. "Plus it's Friday. I guess sometime next week."

The next morning I got an empty jam jar from the cabinet under the stove. I put it in the brown bag with an apple and orange. I felt sick to my stomach. Was that a sign of pregnancy?

Waiting over the weekend was torture. I hardly ate and lay awake worrying. I told my friends I had a sore throat and stayed home all weekend praying that my period would come. And it did come, finally, on Monday morning, eleven days late. I was so relieved. At the Nutrition break, I found Lenny. I expected him to throw his arms around me and twirl me in the air. But instead he dropped his head and looked down at his black loafers.

"I thought you would be happy," I said. He looked up, then off, toward the ocean. The cool sea air chilled my bare legs and I shivered. I could hear seagulls cawing. "I think we should take a break," Lenny finally said.

"From each other?" I asked, incredulous.

"Yeah," he said. Then he looked me in the eye. "This was really scary Mary Lee. I'm not ready to be a father."

The bell rang. Lenny turned. I grabbed his hand. He pulled away. I watched him walk away. I wanted to run after him but stopped, not wanting to make a fool of myself like I did in first grade, when my father carried me onto the bus, kicking and screaming. I wasn't seven-years-old, even if I did feel as powerless as a little kid. I took a deep breath and went to my class.

That night Lenny called and officially broke up with me. I stopped eating. My appetite just vanished. I couldn't focus on homework, friends, or TV. After two weeks Mother took me to a psychologist in Beverly Hills. The therapist's first name was Lenny. Some sort of omen? I told him about my nightmares—trying to run from "bad guys" and suddenly my leg would fall off. I'd lose my balance, stumble and fall into a puddle of blood.

Dr. Lenny explained that this was a natural occurrence after having been in such a symbiotic relationship. There was nothing wrong with me. I just had a broken heart. It would take time to heal. He said I should go out with friends, stay busy.

So reluctantly I did. I hoped that Lenny would miss me and we'd get back together again. Some of Lenny's friends seemed glad I was available. I went out with several of them, to movies and dances, and made out a little, but never let them go very far. I just needed to go out, be social, and dance with my girlfriends.

After a few weeks Lenny called and said he missed me. He wanted to see me but thought it best if we did things with our friends.It was safer if we didn't spend time alone. So we went to parties and movies at the Bay Theater, but I never stayed over at his house again, and after our dates he'd bring me right home. No more parking on Latimer Road.

One March night, Lenny took me down to State Beach to watch the grunion run. Little silver fish gleamed in the moonlight, flopping all along the shoreline. I sat on a damp beach towel, shivering while others scooped the poor creatures up in buckets. Afterwards Lenny kissed me goodnight at the door. His kiss tasted like the ocean.

In April, Lenny's friend William invited me to a double—feature at the Bay Theater, *Send Me No Flowers* and *Father Goose*. We made out a little. He was an okay kisser, but nothing like Lenny.

I continued to take dance lessons at the Riviera Country Club but afterwards I'd walk home with Kathie, have a snack and then she'd take me home because I still had not gotten my driver's license. I didn't hang out with Lenny's sister anymore or spend time at her house, unless it was for a Dupree club meeting. My club mates and I organized garage sales, made posters, went to retirement homes and wrote letters for the elderly residents. We had parties on Saturday nights. I helped write our songs for the semi-annual Song Banquet and awards dinner.

In May I turned sixteen. My sweet sister secretly arranged a kidnap breakfast for me and six of my friends. She called their mothers the night before to ask them to make sure their front doors were unlocked at 7:00 a.m. She bought us all breakfast at Uncle John's Pancake House, then we spent the rest of the day at State Beach, gossiping and shivering in the fog. I wasn't in love. But I was okay. And soon, I would find something else—besides boys—to love.

Chapter 13

I BECOME A DANCER

When school ended in June, Mother said, "Young lady, you're not going to spend another summer lolling on the beach all day. You're either going to summer school or be in a play."

What? I wanted to loll on the beach all day and watch boys surf, then hang out at the Bay Theater or with my girlfriends. This was terrible news.

I didn't have the confidence to audition for a "real" play, even though I'd been entertaining my parents and their friends since I was little, and performed with my friends in school talent shows.

For "Color Cotton Day"—an all-girl talent show, performed before all the girls at school, (the boys must have been off doing sports, or something), I created a skit for me and three of my friends. I got the idea from an album my parents had of silent movie

118

music. A dramatic harpsichord piece was perfect for a story about Simon Lagree—played by me in top hat and drawn-on handle-bar mustache, kidnapping the pretty young girl (Marilyn) from her grandmother (Julie). Subsequently she'd be rescued by Dudley Do-right (Joanne in bowler hat). I had the lighting crew flicker the lights and it really did look like an old-time movie.

I loved performing for family and classmates, but the idea of auditioning in front of professionals, to be in a production with total strangers, who were way more experienced and talented that I was just too scary. So when Mother gave me the choice, I solemnly replied, "Summer school."

Pali High didn't have summer school at this time. The closest school was University High near U.C.L.A. (where my sister had gone because Pali wasn't built until her senior year). Mother drove me over to "Uni", an old school that took up a city block. I found the gum-stained sidewalks and apartment buildings across the street depressing. I was used to Pali's wide, open campus, nestled in Temescal Canyon, with spectacular views of the Malibu Mountains and the Pacific Ocean. The dark, musty corridors of forty-year-old Uni creeped me out. I could hear car horns and police sirens. The *pachuco* boys with their greased back hair were scary. And the girls with ratted, sprayed hair looked cheap. By 1965 my friends and I were going for a more "natural" look. We stopped using hairspray and started combing lemon juice or watered-down peroxide through our hair before we went to the beach, to give the sun a little extra boost. We were beach girls, not city girls. Our campus smelled of eucalyptus and the ocean, not smog and cigarettes.

"I guess I'll try the play," I told Mother, assuming that I'd have a terrible audition and be rejected. Then what would I do?

Mother had seen in the paper a casting call for a musical at the Bluth Brothers Theater in Culver City. When she called she was told the play had been cast, but to bring me by and they'd take a look at me. The play was *High Spirits*, the musical of Noel Coward's comedy *Blithe Spirit*.

Don Bluth was, and is, an animator. He worked for Walt Disney Studios for many years before becoming a director. His official website states: *He opened the Bluth Brothers Theater with his younger brother Fred in an old supermarket in Culver City. They produced musical plays with local talent for two to three years . . . Often Don was the musician, playing the piano. One attendee stated it was like an old movie musical where kids decide to put a show on in a barn.*

I loved the diverse cast, which ranged from high school students, like myself, to actors in their forties. There was no stage, per se, just a curtain with a big floor space in front, surrounded on three sides by banked seats.

That first night Mother sat in the audience while I joined the dancers and learned the rollicking opening number, "Give Me a Bike." Madame Arcati, an eccentric middle-aged medium in gypsy garb, sings about loving to ride her bike in the English countryside. Singers and dancers back her up. My dance partner, Jim, rode in on a bike, set the kick-stand and stood beside it. That was my cue to dance onto stage. I needed to build momentum as I approached, so that by the time I reached Jim, he could grasp me by the waist, and in one swift motion, gracefully lift me over the bike and set me down. I can't tell you how many nights—at least half—my foot got caught on the bike and poor Jim struggled to disentangle me. Yet the director never changed the choreography.

Each night, waiting back stage to come on, my heart pounded so hard I thought I'd faint. On the nights our maneuver worked and I was whisked over the handlebars, I breathed easy and enjoyed the rest of the show. When we screwed up I tried to laugh it off and carry on.

I developed a crush on a twenty-five-year-old dancer—tall, dark, curly brown hair. I Googled him recently and I found that he went on to be a successful set designer. Back then he and I spent hours backstage, making out.

In July he invited the cast to a party at his apartment. The courtyard had a pool. While everyone else was swimming and eating barbecued hamburgers, he and I made out upstairs. He stretched out on the couch and I sat on the floor. We kissed and kissed until everyone had left including my ride. By the time he took me home at dawn, my lips were so swollen I could hardly talk. I only drank water that night, but felt as light-headed and happy as if I'd had champagne.

On Wednesday, August 11th, I woke up with a fever of 103. I was bummed out that I'd miss rehearsal. I wheeled our black and white TV into my room and laid on my bed to listlessly watch Dick Clarke's *Where the Action Is*. Suddenly the regular programming was interrupted by a newsman announcing that riots had broken out in Watts.

All I knew about Watts was that it was somewhere near downtown L.A. I'd read an article about the Watts Towers in the L.A. Times: an Italian immigrant named Sam Rodia took thirty-four years (1921-1955) to complete—by hand—amazing pointy metal towers that he decorated with ceramics and glass. Now the newscaster was calling Watts a "ghetto" a word I'd never heard before, which meant that it was Colored, and poor.

My high school was all white, Christians and Jews. These were the days before mandatory school busing. We had one Japanese-American girl, and I knew two girls whose families were Persian: one (who would be voted the most beautiful girl in our graduating class) was a niece of the Shah, and I'd been to the other girl's house, where the floors were covered in beautiful dark red rugs. Her grandmother, who spoke no English, served us a milky rose-scented custard.

But the only Colored people I knew growing up were Bea, our elderly maid, and after she retired, Mr. Middlebrooks who owned a three-man cleaning crew that came every other Saturday morning. I didn't like the inconvenience of having to be up and out of my bedroom early but my annoyance was tempered by my crush on Leonard, who was probably in his early twenties, 6' 4" with muscular nut-brown arms and a slow, easy manner. He wore a short-sleeved navy blue shirt, navy slacks and black shoes with thick rubber soles. I'd sit on the kitchen stool, hair disheveled, hunched over my bowl of Wheat Chex, wearing the green quilt robe Mother had made me, with its flattering scoop-neck, and watch Leonard rhythmically run his mop in big circles over our terrazzo floors.

121

My family liked Sidney Portier, Harry Belafonte and Bill Cosby. *I Spy* was the coolest show on TV, with Cosby playing a hip detective. A school friend's father produced the show. I always hoped she'd introduce me, but we weren't *that* good of friends, so it never happened.

One day, when a neighbor up the street told Mother that she had her Colored maid sit in the back seat when she drove her home, Mother said, "Oh, you mean you chauffeur her?" I was proud of her for that remark. Our family was for equality and got tears in our eyes when we saw Freedom Riders in the south, or heard Dr. Martin Luther King's inspiring speeches.

My biggest fear until now had been wild fires. I'd gone with my father up to Inspiration Point in Santa Monica when he photographed flames galloping over the mountains toward Pacific Palisades, and I'd witnessed the charred remains of Susie and Teresa's grandparents' house burned in the 1958 Malibu fire. On my half-birthday, November 6, 1961, Paul Revere Junior High was evacuated because of the Bel-Air fire that came within blocks of our campus. Several of my friends lost their homes.

But this conflagration wasn't an act of nature. The Watts riots were people destroying their own neighborhoods! Seeing images of windows smashed and fires blazing I felt scared. Would these angry hoodlums come over to the West Side and break windows in our shops? It made no sense. Why destroy your own neighborhood? I'm sure my parents tried to assure me that we were perfectly safe in our little canyon, but I wasn't so sure.

It turned out that a black motorist had been arrested for drunk driving. The white cop would not let his brother drive his car home. Onlookers started throwing rocks. Soon a crowd had gathered and shop windows were broken. A racist remark by one of the white police, that people were acting like "monkeys in a zoo" fueled more violence. It went on for days. In the end, thirty-four people died, over a 1,000 were injured and more than 3,000 people were arrested.

I got up to get a glass of water and when I got back into bed the news had switched to the latest battles of the Viet Nam war—both over there, where the jungle was ablaze with napalm, and at home where student protests were happening at more and more universities.

Just a month before, my mother and I had gotten into a heated discussion at the dinner table. I defended the Johnson administration, saying we were simply aiding our anti-communist allies. Mother gave me a dressing-down and let me know in no uncertain terms that this was completely different from World War II. Because my parents had been huge Kennedy supporters, they didn't put the blame on him for getting the U.S. involved in Southeast Asia in the first place. They considered LBJ a swaggering good-ole boy Texan and didn't like him, in spite of his social programs they supported. They thought he had no class. *Life* magazine ran a big picture of him pulling up his shirt to show off his gall bladder scar.

Popular music was changing, reflecting the times. At school a girl two-years older than I, quoted Bob Dylan lyrics and turned me on to his album *Freewheelin.'* He had a terrible voice but fantastic lyrics that I memorized by playing his record over and over on my little portable record player. I still loved the Beatles and will always remember their first appearance on Ed Sullivan in January 1964. But I also started listening to Joan Baez and Woody Guthrie whose songs gave voice to a social movement. My sister brought home a button from an anti-war protest that said *Stop the War Now* which I proudly wore on my favorite plaid blazer. She also gave me that famous poster: *War is not healthy for children or other living things.*

So, with all the unrest and uncertainty of race issues and the war—not to mention growing unrest between my parents—I was happy to escape to the Bluth Brothers Theater five nights a week, to dance and sing and make out with a twenty-five year old man. Plus, I could "loll on the beach all day" with my friends, after all.

My parents said I could throw a cast party when *High Spirits* ended. Everyone came in costume and entertained—telling jokes, dancing, singing. I lip-synced to "Don't Rain on My Parade" from *Funny Girl,* and of course my dad took pictures.

Two weeks after school started in the fall of 1965, my friend Gretta threw herself a birthday party on Saturday night, September 25. She lived on an estate in Brentwood, a large property behind tall hedges with a big lawn and tennis court. Her father didn't want kids walking on the tennis court but that's where everyone hung out. Some of us snuck off to make out under the tall sycamores or in the back seats of our boyfriend's cars.

THE SLUMBER PARTY

The boys came
wearing tennis shoes
carrying beer cans.

Girls were ready
in our baby dolls
wanting them to want us.

They did for a little while
on the couch,
in the back of vans.

And then we were just girls again
with hickeys and swollen lips
wanting more—
having to wait
the rest of our lives.

At the party I met Josh, an artist, who was a year older than I, but seemed so much more mature. He drove a 1957 dark green Chevy station wagon with a light green tail gate on which he'd painted *A Love Supreme*, the title of a John Coltrane album, in red script. Josh was the first person I knew who listened to jazz. I was thrilled when he picked *me* to make out with. Soon we were dating.

JOSH

Down in the hollow
of Mandeville Canyon
the light in his bedroom
was golden as honey

A Love Supreme
flowed all around us
saxophone soothing
as his pencil moved

he liked my hands
wanted to draw them
I liked his broad, flat
ruddy face

I was so small beside him
as he drew me and drew me
into him on his narrow bed

his hot blood mingled with
the scent of Bay Rum

my own blood
moved in slow confusion
my mind gathered and lost thoughts
as if they were moths
easily damaged
by being touched.

Josh sometimes took weekend drives up the coast to paint and
draw. He didn't mind if I went out with other guys. And when he
went away to college, he'd often visit me when he came home. I
can't say I was *in love* with Josh, but I liked him a lot. I admired and
respected him and am sad I've lost track of him. The last time I saw

him in 1970, in San Francisco, he was raising chickens and selling their guano to strawberry farmers.

On November 6, 1965—my half birthday and the fourth anniversary of the Bel Air fire, I had a date William, Lenny's surfer-friend. I was going to cook dinner for my parents first (stuffed, rolled flank steak) and write a report for my Home Economics class. I used my mother's heavy, orange, Dutch oven. The dinner was actually quite good.

After I cleaned up the kitchen, I dressed in new hip-hugger bell bottoms, white with little olive-green flowers. I wore soft Italian olive-green shoes, as comfortable as slippers. I wore a pale orange "poor boy" top—a fitted, ribbed, short-sleeved tee that showed off my figure. My long blonde hair fell to my shoulders and flipped up naturally. I brushed my bangs and put on lots of mascara. I looked in the bathroom drawer and saw my flavored lipsticks that Lenny loved to kiss off. I couldn't bring myself to throw them away, but I didn't want to wear them with anyone else, either. I put on some of my mother's coral Maybelline instead.

William arrived in his light-yellow Fiat, the smallest car I'd ever seen. He said we were going to a party. That car was so small, and he drove so fast! I was relieved when we finally stopped.

I got out of the car and breathed deeply. Yum, night blooming jasmine, a delicious smell that calmed me. When William got out, he reached behind the back seat and pulled out a six pack of Budweiser. I didn't see any lights on in the house. I followed him around the side, through a gate, to a little pool-house. The night smelled of chlorine and fresh cut grass. The door was unlocked.

Inside, dim light filtered in through curtain-less windows revealing no furniture, just a mattress on the floor with blue-and-white ticking, and a radio. William turned on the radio. Barry McGuire's raspy voice filled the small room, "*Were on the eve of destruction . . .*"

I sat on the mattress. William reached into his pocket and took out a bottle opener. He opened a bottle of Bud and handed it to me but I shook my heard. He took a swig. He put his arm around me. He kissed me. He tasted like beer.

ALLOWED

We were allowed
carrots and celery before dinner
we were allowed
to take them
out of the refrigerator ourselves
and wash them under the tap.
We were allowed
to collect chewed gum
and holy cards.
We were allowed
to dress up
like senoritas.
We were even allowed
to promise ourselves to God.

How lucky we were
that we were not accosted
by gardeners
the way my mother was
accosted by a gardener
in off-white overalls
who bent over so she could see
he wore nothing underneath.
He held her hands
and stroked
her pretty blond hair.

The man on the beach
did not touch me,
he was far away
far enough to throw a stone
if I had wanted to throw a stone
at his horrible grimace
when he took down his pants.
That horrible smile.

How lucky we were
that the men who loved us
stayed away from us.
Our fathers wore khaki pants
and short sleeved shirts
that showed their
strong tan arms.
We stroked their arms
but they never stroked back.
They were so careful
not to love us
too much.
They were almost
like stone.

How lucky I was
that it was someone who knew me
who knew my heart was broken
by his best friend,
my boyfriend's best friend
a surfer in a little tiny Fiat
that was so small
it scared me.

He drove so fast
through Benedict Canyon
and Lauren Canyon
and Mandeville Canyon
looking for a place
to rape me.
But it wasn't called
rape back then
it was called
being stupid
not knowing some guys
don't listen when you say

please
no
please
don't
some guys don't care
if you still love their best friend
because they have beer
and a radio
and a little tiny car
so small
it feels like
riding in
a baby carriage
but it is not
baby blood
it is my blood
and my fault
so I won't tell anyone
ever.

How lucky I was
that I was allowed
to go on dates
in little tiny cars
and not have to tell
about it afterwards.
I was allowed
to sit in the bathtub
bleeding
and no one
had to know

Was I a slut now? I kept this secret for twenty-three years until I wrote the above poem in 1988.

Chapter 14

1966

I knew beatniks smoked weed and social comedians like Lenny Bruce shot "horse" or "smack" but so far I didn't know anyone who used drugs. My parents didn't drink much. Sometimes if Mother had to go to Hollywood to drop off color film to be processed, and deal with traffic and heat, she'd say, "I need a drink!" and make herself a Scotch and water. She treated it like medicine.

On our trip to Europe my father developed a taste for *Liebfraumilch* and would sometimes have a glass of the sweet white wine with dinner. In fact, to encourage my appetite, he'd sometimes water it down for me, as European parents did.

But I never saw my parents drunk. They were very health conscious. My dad was a member of Lyle Fox Gym in Pacific

Palisades and in our junior year, Kathie and I joined, too. Our physiology teacher, Mrs. Herbst, taught us about nutrition. I can see her tall and imposing, intoning like Julia Child, "I don't have white sugar in my house!"

As a special gift to Mrs. Herbst I asked my dad to take before-and-after pictures of me and Kathie. In the first one we rubbed eye shadow under our eyes, mussed our hair and stood slumped in our leotards, with our stomachs pooching out. The caption said, "Before we took your class we didn't know anything about health and nutrition." Inside, we stood straight with our stomachs sucked in and fresh-scrubbed faces, smiling brightly. The caption read, "Thank you Mrs. Herbst!" So, even though I had friends who might sneak drinks from their parents' liquor cabinets, I had no desire to.

However, a few weeks shy of my seventeenth birthday I did accidentally get drunk. I'd been dating Bill, a star pole-vaulter who lived nearby on Latimer Road. We weren't in love, but he was cute and easy to be with. We'd go out on Friday nights, to home football games, or to movies.

The Saturday we went to the Olympic Drive In, *The Ghost and Mr. Chicken*, starring Don Knotts was playing. Kathie was between boyfriends at the time, so we double-dated with her, and Bill's friend Randy.

Bill opened the glove compartment and pulled out a flask. He poured rum into our cokes. We made out during the movie and I felt kind of dizzy. As soon as he dropped me off I ran into the house and threw up in the models' dressing room toilet. That was the last time I drank in high school, and I never drank rum again.

Three-and-a-half years of wearing braces had produced straight teeth. I still wore a retainer at night, and Dr. Bench had accidentally broken off the inside prong of my left eye tooth when he removed the bands—"Just go next door and have it filed down," he said—but the worst was over and my self confidence had returned.

131

I was still thin, ninety-nine pounds, but, as Mother had taught me, had good proportion: 34-24-34. Sun, lemon juice and peroxide had turned my mousy hair to glimmering blond. It fell softly to my shoulders. I'd gained theater experience in a summer stock musical and school talent shows. As musical director of our YWCA sponsored club I'd won the trophy for writing lyrics to popular songs at the annual Song Banquets. I'd been posing for my father since I was born. So now I felt it was time to become a professional model. After all, my parents had connections in Hollywood, why not use them?

Mother thought we should start at the top, with the Mary Webb Davis agency, on the Sunset Strip in Hollywood, which represented high-paid, high-fashion models who appeared on *Vogue* and *Harpers Bazaar*, not the sort of glamour models my parents usually photographed. Because I was petite and young—an *engenue*—my dream was to be in *Seventeen Magazine*.

We splurged on a 14" x 20" leather-bound portfolio to hold a variety of black and white enlargements: a head shot, with hair up, applying a dab of cream to my cheek; standing straight-on, in my bell bottoms and poor-boy shirt; looking dreamy, leaning against the trunk of a sycamore; an action shot of my hair flying out as I spun around in a *High Spirits* dance scene.

Mother and I went to the appointment. I wasn't nervous. I felt like my life was really beginning now, that great things were in store for me.

The walls of the waiting room displayed blow ups almost as big as movie posters, of gorgeous models. I recognized Susie Parker, Jean Shrimpton, and Veruschka, but didn't yet know the pretty blond—Sybil Shepherd.

Mary Webb Davis was an intimidating, no-nonsense business woman in a sleek suit. When we placed the photo album on her desk, she leafed through it and pronounced, "You'll have to file your teeth."

The rest of the interview is a blur. My mind went numb at the thought of more mouth torture. Yes, sure, my two front teeth were a bit longer than the others but the idea of a dentist sticking his big meaty hands in my mouth and filing them down . . . I visualized a screeching machine the size of a belt sander and felt sick.

A few years later Lauren Hutton would be on the cover of *Vogue* with a huge gap between her two front teeth. But for the most part models were expected to have perfectly proportioned bodies and faces, and teeth uniform as kernels of corn. Stunning Isabella Rossellini, in her memoir *Some of Me*, says that it was not until late in her modeling career that Lancôme finally stopped making her use mortician's wax to fill in the chip on a front tooth she broke as a little girl, when her brother threw a telephone at her.

I hardly heard the rest of what Mary Webb Davis said. Something about being too short, and my face was too thin. Models should have wide cheekbones.

As we drove home I stared out the window, completely deflated. Mother prattled on about my other talents, my love of the theater, where, after all you didn't need to look perfect. And I liked to write didn't I? She was trying to be encouraging but her words didn't fill my empty feeling.

Mother pulled the car into the garage. My dad was talking to one of his workers. They were examining a new batch of aluminum bodies for his custom made Gowlandflex cameras. Bellows and lenses were scattered on the worktable.

"Well?" he said as we got out of the car. Mother just heaved a big sigh.

"There are other agencies . . ." she started to tell me, but I ignored her and went into the house. My black cat was lounging on the couch. I picked him up and carried him into my room. I laid on the bed, put him on my chest and looked into his dark yellow eyes. I stroked his face, feeling his magnificent wide cheek bones.

Years later, when I was in my thirties, my father gave my chin an affectionate squeeze and said "How can any man want to kiss that little skinny face?" Ice ran through me and took me back to that afternoon when I was sixteen and realized no matter what I did, I was just not quite good enough.

Mary Lee Gowland

PHOTOGRAPHER'S KISS

My father grabs my face
and bends to plant
a big wet kiss on my cheek.
He puckers my face the way
some people scold disobedient dogs
and says, "How can any man
want to kiss
such a little skinny face?"

I use to think
I wanted to be a model,
but I found out
I have the wrong bone structure.
No amount of fill-in flash
will compensate for this deformity.

And yet, many men have kissed me.
Sometimes I thought their breath was mine.
I have often gotten lost in kisses
wishing I could push out from inside
make myself large, take in
not just tongues and lips and breath but
the whole body, an entire being, the same
gender as my tall thin father
who doesn't say
"Your face is perfect, beyond beautiful."
        this face he gave me
to help me overcome
the shape of failing him
of not being like
the women he photographs
with rolls and rolls
of black and white film.

I wrote that in 1988, in Brenda Hillman's Workshop at the Squaw Valley Writers' Conference. When I got back from the conference I invited my parents to my condo, the first and only time they ever came to my house to eat. I made a pasta salad. My father asked "Where's the rest of the dinner?"

Mother asked if I would read something I wrote at the conference. I chose that poem. When I finished, I looked up and saw my mother had tears in her eyes. My father said, "Did you write anything else about me?"

I looked at Mother and just shook my head.

In June 1966 Mother saw a notice in the Los Angeles Times: the City of Beverly Hills, with the City of Santa Monica and the Los Angeles Department of Parks and Recreation, was going to stage a production of the Rogers and Hart musical, *Babes in Arms.* Kathie and I decided to try out.

Whereas my mom had called Bluth Brothers Theater the summer before and almost magically gotten me into *Blithe Spirit*, this would be a real audition. I'd have to *sing*. Alone. On the stage of the gigantic, 16,000 square foot Santa Monica Civic Auditorium. Gulp.

Kathie drove us in her VW station wagon. The piano accompanist was Craig Saffan who went on to become an award winning film, stage and TV composer. I sang *The Lady is a Tramp* in a thin, reedy voice barely audible in the back of the auditorium. They cast me as Debby, with no speaking lines. Kathie actually had several lines as Libby. Both of us were dancers.

In the opening number there was a move where we extended our arms, turned, extended (facing upstage), then turned again downstage, as we sang *"Play day is done, there's a place in the sun . . ."* and almost every night, Kathie went in the wrong direction.

She'd catch my eye and give me a wide surprised look. I always thought she did it on purpose, to make me laugh.

A lot of the cast were from Beverly Hills High School, including the lead Michael Lembeck, son of comic actor Harvey Lembeck; and Jerry Peck, son of Hollywood choreographer Steven Peck.

Kathie fell in love with" Lembeck". Our friend Joanne, who had a summer job at the Brentwood Country Mart and no desire to do theater, fell in love with Jerry.

I was happy, dating several nice guys, hanging out at the beach or going to the gym during the day, and to rehearsals at night, letting my friends chauffer me around. My parents had planned to give me the 1959 Mercedes 150 when I turned sixteen and buy themselves a new one. When Ann turned sixteen they bought her a cute little white MG roadster, with red leather interior.

I had my learner's permit and Mother had given me some lessons. Plus, I'd taken the mandatory Drivers Ed class at school, struggling to parallel park a huge Ford. But I didn't really want to drive. It was much more fun to be picked up by either Kathie, who always loved to drive—she started at fourteen, taking her parents Borgward without permission—or my boyfriends. So, although I could have gotten my license a year earlier, I just didn't want to. Besides, I certainly didn't want to drive my parent's seven-year-old car with all the awful memories of that trip to Europe. When I was finally ready, I'd want a Volkswagen Beetle, which was what all my friends wanted.

On August 11th, I was in my room, still in my nightgown, listening to *Man of La Mancha* to drown out the sound of quarreling in the kitchen. It was the same old stuff: Mother was sick of my dad running around. He'd go out and not come back till one or two in the morning. She would be "worried sick" by the time he returned.

But something was different this time. It wasn't just about having her feelings hurt, or fearing a jealous boyfriend would shoot him. This time it was about money.

Most of the girls my father dated were happy just to have their picture taken by a famous photographer. He was always very thrifty and didn't spend money on himself, let alone other women. I don't think he ever carried much cash. His wallet was a rubber band. Mother ran the office and handled the money. (She taught me how to do a spread sheet). They had only one checking account that was used for business and personal expenses. If my dad wanted money he had to ask her for it.

Evidently, from the yelling in the kitchen, I learned my dad had started to spend a lot of money. The culprit was a German stewardess he had met on one of their overseas trips. She liked fur coats.

"If you're going to spend thousands of dollars, I will too!" I heard Mother shout. Then a rap on my bedroom door. Before I could open it, she had pushed the door open.

"Get dressed!" she commanded, eyes blazing. "We're going to go buy you a car!" My stomach turned over.

"I don't want a car," I started to say but she cut me off.

"I've had it up to here with you two," she said slashing her hand across her neck. I could see her veins pulsing. "You're seventeen years old, it's time you grow up, or you're going to end up like your father, who thinks he can get away with anything he wants just because he's good looking and has a camera hanging around his neck! I'm putting my foot down!" She turned and stomped back into the kitchen.

As I took off my nightie and stood staring into my closet I could hear her rant: "Your mother named you Peter after Peter Pan so you'd never grow up. Well you never did. But I'm tired of being your mother. If you're going to spend money on other women I'm going to spend money too, half of everything we have is mine and I've certainly earned it."

We went to Santa Monica Motors to look at Volkswagen Beetles. Because I was depressed I selected beige. Mother wrote a check for $2,100 and I drove the car home. Eventually I would grow to love that little Bug. Four years later, when my boyfriend and I moved to Mount Shasta, my father built a wooden rack for the roof that held everything we owned.

In July 1966, Kathie and I entered the Miss Pacific Palisades contest. We and the other contestants had two photographs in the Palisadian Post. On the Fourth of July we all got to ride on a fire engine down Sunset Boulevard and wave to the flag-waving spectators on the sidewalk. The parade ended at Palisades Park where the pagent was held. Kathie and I were extremely disappointed that neither of us won.

Performances of *Babes in Arms* were held over three weekends—at Plummer Park in Los Angeles, at Beverly Hills High School and at Santa Monica High School. We rehearsed for several weeks at Beverly High, and then held a technical and a dress rehearsal at each of the other locations before the weekend shows. Because flash wasn't allowed during performances, the directors let my father come to our dress rehearsals and take many rolls of black-and-white 35mm film. It was very kind of him to make 8"10" prints for the cast, as well.

There is nothing more thrilling than being back stage when the orchestra tunes up. Your heart races. You think you'll never remember your lines, or steps, or cues. And then the overture begins and the auditorium fills with music and nerves turn into pure electric energy. The curtain goes up, you rush on stage, find your place. When you look out toward the audience all you see is white light but you know there are people sitting in the dark watching, listening. Then the stage is filled with other bodies moving around you, and with you, and it's almost like being swept up in an ocean of music, rhythm, joy. I loved every minute of it: hasty costume changes, quick make-up repairs, huddling with friends before we went on stage, the finale where the entire stage was full of singing and dancing, and last, the curtain call, when the house lights come up and you can look to see your friends in the audience.

Toward the end of the play's run, Lembeck and Jerry's friend Rick came to a performance. I liked him. He was fun and funny. Soon we were hanging out with Kathie and Lembeck, Joanne and Jerry, spending all our free time together. The boys would start college in the fall. Lembeck enrolled to USC Film School and went on to be an actor and director. Jerry followed in his dad's footsteps, becoming a choreographer and *restauranteur.* Rick, became a businessman.

On October 19th Rick came to my house in his new 1966 white Chevy Impala which was perfect for the six of us to triple-date. We had a lot of fun that fall. The boys came to our prom. We went to many movies in Westwood, or grabbed a bite to eat at Cantor's Deli on Fairfax. Then we'd all go back to Lembeck's house, pair off and make out in separate bedrooms. We all wondered, but never asked, if the other couples were "going all the way."

There was one other "Y" sponsored club in our grade, the Shendores. Our only real competition with each other was at the fall and spring Song Banquets. Otherwise we went to each other's parties or hung out together at the beach. Someone got the idea to have a football game between the two clubs on the field of Paul Revere Junior High. We'd all have to climb the fence on a Saturday afternoon.

I had no desire to play football, so I said I would be the Dupree cheerleader. A few weeks before the big game, practices were held at Palisades Park. Players on Pali's varsity football team coached us. By the day of the game, we were ready to go.

I had a hard time climbing over the chain-link fence, I didn't want to rip my tight white bellbottoms. Other girls, more athletic than I, wearing shorts, scrambled over. We actually had a pretty good crowd of onlookers, cheering from the sidelines. The two teams positioned themselves on the field and the referee blew the whistle.

Immediately one of the Shendore players tackled Kathie and threw her to the ground. This was definitely against the rules—it was supposed to be a *touch* football game. Kathie screamed in pain and didn't get up. Boys rushed to her aid. She held her arm and kept saying, "My shoulder! My shoulder!"

I sat with her on a bench. Joanne joined us. "I think I dislocated my shoulder!" she said. Joanne and I looked at each other.

Kathie was known for exaggerating, which as an adult has made her a successful writer. But when we were in elementary school, Mother had once said, "I don't like you playing with her, she won't look me in the eye."

The thing was: Kathie's stories were so interesting, did we care if they were true or not? She had come to California when she was ten, from the East Coast and had an air of sophistication about her. She'd worn her hair in two long, brown braids and wore dark socks with her oxfords. I liked her right away. I liked her even more when

I went to her house and saw how many books she had, shelves and shelves lining the walls.

Her father was a short, serious lawyer who wore suits and smoked cigars. In the entry of their house was a four-foot-tall white Styrofoam eagle, the Pan Am logo, for he was an executive there. He was a well-connected Democrat and knew many famous people in New York and Washington DC.

Her tall, willowy mother had been a model in New York before marrying. Her father was Jewish. Her mother was Mormon. She had a black poodle named Lizzie and a sister, two years younger, named Marie. Their house had a *lanai*, and a huge collection of LPs, including lots of Broadway shows. They were the coolest family I knew.

Sitting on the bench with Kathie moaning, Joanne and I gave each other a look. Was she really hurt, or did she just want to get out of the game? We decided we better take her to the hospital. UCLA was just a few miles away.

With a lot of grunting and groaning several boys helped push Kathie up and over the fence. Joanne and I dropped her off at the emergency room and went to Ships where we sat in an orange, vinyl booth and ate English muffins that we could toast at our table. Then we walked around Westwood Village looking in shop windows at A-line skirts and tried on pointed flats at C.H. Baker Shoes. At Bullock's we spritzed each other with Shalimar Cologne and tested lipsticks. At the record store, in listening booths we played the Lovin' Spoonful and the Beach Boys. Finally we decided we should go back and see how Kathie was doing.

She was in a full body cast. She had broken her collar bone. Her mother was on her way to pick her up.

During her convalescence, Kathie sat propped in bed, in her book-lined room. Friends visited and brought the latest gossip. Lembeck visited every day and their relationship deepened. Ricky and I drifted apart. My friends were obsessed about applying to colleges. Kathie wanted me to apply to Emerson College in Boston where she had been accepted. Boston! That was *way* too far away for me. Heidi was going up to UC Santa Barbara, but my grades weren't that good. Besides I didn't even take the SAT.

You see, neither of my parents had gone to college. In fact, my father dropped out of Hollywood High his senior year to work in movies. When he married my mom, she made him go back and get his GED. And yet, they were successful, doing what they loved and having a great life. So, I didn't give college much thought, figuring I might get work in the movies, or equity theater. And if worse came to worst, I could take classes at Santa Monica College like Ann had. She met Frank, a quarterback, there and together they had my darling niece, Tracy.

I concentrated on enjoying my senior year. I played Polly in a school production of Bertolt Brecht's *Three Penny Opera*. My mediocre singing voice was fine for Kurt Weill's dissonant songs. I loved my photography class and doing "service" with my Y Club.

On New Year's Eve, my friends and I were at Lembeck's parent's house. But this time I was making out with a different friend of his, a cool ex-New Yorker. I felt a sense of dread as the clock struck midnight, ushering in a year full of change. I worried about my parents, were they heading for divorce? I worried about the escalating Vietnam War. I worried about race riots. What would become of the world? What would become of me? I felt like I was falling off a cliff and had no idea where I would land.

Chapter 15

I BECOME A POET

I entered 1967 with a sense of dread: in six months I'd be out of high school with no plans to go to college, and my parents seemed about to get divorced. On two occasions Mother rented my father an apartment and told him to leave, but he refused. She even took all his clothes out of the closet and put them in the car. But he just carried them back into the house.

Once, when we were just finishing breakfast, Mother got so mad she threw a cup she was rinsing into the sink, "I can't take it anymore. You're making me crazy!" she cried.

My dad, who had been sitting at the counter, got off his stool and came around to the sink. Mother took a step back.

"You want to break dishes?" he asked calmly. Then he reached into the dishwasher and slowly took out plates, cups and saucers and threw them, one by one, the length of the house. They flew past the living room toward the studio, bouncing and breaking on the hard terrazzo. I cringed and stepped back into the alcove by the pantry and put my hands over my ears.

"Stop it!" Mother screamed at him.

Finally he did. He gave her a cold stare and left the house. Mother sat on the little stool under the phone and put her head in her hands, sobbing. I went to the broom closet and got a dust pan and cleaned up the mess.

After these sorts of outbursts, things would settle down for a while. Their work life was at its peak. The Rigid Tool calendar was a huge job that took months. Raquel Welch was one of the first models. Mother would call various model agencies and tell them she was looking for wholesome, "girl-next-door" types. When the company representative arrived from back east, he, my mom and dad would go through the photos and select about fifty to be interviewed in person. Mother would drive him around looking at various locations.

Twelve locations had to be found: private homes, the beach, a park, our backyard, the studio. In the 1950s it was a lot easier to use the public beach but by the late 1960s you had to have a permit. Plus, public places invited gawking crowds. So, more and more they asked friends and neighbors if they could use their yards—for a fee, of course.

Mother also bought two or three bathing suits per model. My dad created sets for the studio. The earliest calendars were simple and kind of corny—some fake lawn, a bit of picket fence. But over the years the sets became more elaborate.

One of the most amazing things my dad designed and built was a waterfall he constructed for the pool. His assistant stood on a ladder and spilled buckets of water down the fake rock background. And I remember a faux boulder my dad made from chicken wire and covered in *papier maché*, then painted brown. He could put it in the trunk of the car and take it to the beach. I thought it looked like a giant baked potato.

My parents had a series of workers over the years, and most of them became like part of the family. Many were photography students at Santa Monica College. They helped on photo shoots, lugging cameras, reflectors and props across the sand for a shoot at the beach. They developed and printed pictures in the darkrooms. When my dad invented his line of Gowlandflex cameras he needed machinists to create the aluminum bodies and assemble the finished camera—lenses, bellows, mirrors. My mom needed an assistant, too, to help her in the office. She'd gotten the idea to advertise their photo catalogs as posing guides. So every day the mail brought in checks from all over the country, even the world, from amateurs wanting to learn from the master. My mom called this their "bread and butter business."

Of all their many employees there was only one who stole from them and had to be let-go. What I remember most about her is the day my parents were off shooting stills on the set of the movie version of *Bye Bye Birdie*. This clepto-secretary told me my eye brows needed plucking and volunteered to do it. "Beauty takes pain," she said as tears streamed down my cheeks.

Most of my mother's friends thought she should just divorce my father. Let him have his German stewardess. Mother was torn. Her heart was broken every time he spent time away from her, with another woman.

But our neighbor Pat pointed out all she would lose: her livelihood, her home, her family, plus the man she loved. To me Mother once sighed and said, "Some men drink, and some men gamble, and some men run around."

It wasn't as if my father didn't love her. He *adored* her. He never stopped being attracted to her. He was very affectionate. I remember a lot of hugging in the kitchen. He just wanted to be with other women too.

Mother theorized that he was making up for the affection he didn't get as a child because his parents divorced when he was only two, and his father had custody. His cold, unaffectionate father.

I always thought my father ran around on my mother because he could. His pleasure was more important than the pain he caused her or me or even the girls who had their hearts broken when he dumped them.

When I felt really stressed over all this "parent stuff, I'd call my friend Kathie and say, "I need a pep talk!" She was a good listener and could commiserate because her parents had problems too. How would I live without her when she went to Boston to college? Plus, her father had decided to move the whole family to New York right after graduation. What if I never saw her again? I felt heartsick.

So, in my final year at Pali High, I spent as much time as I could away from home, with my friends at club meetings or rehearsing for school plays. Although I didn't have a steady boyfriend, I always had a date on Saturday night. When things were especially horrible at home I took solace at Heidi's house. It was comforting to know that in the fall Heidi would be at UC Santa Barbara, an hour-and-a-half drive up the coast.

My friend Janet, a redhead, lived in the ritzy neighborhood of Huntington Palisades where large two-story homes were surrounded by sprawling lawns and manicured yards. Very different from cozy Rustic Canyon.

Janet and I liked to ensconce ourselves in her frilly, pink bedroom and read *Seventeen, Vogue* and *Harpers Bazaar*. I remember the first time we saw Twiggy with her huge eyes, accentuated by drawn-on lower eyelashes. She had such long, skinny legs in miniskirts, and short boyish hair.

"She looks like you!" Janet said, "if you cut your hair."

"Come with me!" I said.

"Really? You're going to cut your hair? Now?"

I drove the few blocks to a beauty salon across the street from the Bay Theater.

"Can you please give me a Twiggy cut?" I asked the hairdresser. Suddenly I felt nervous. My mother, or Pat had always cut my hair—except for my experience on Glamour Girl. Could I trust a stranger? Oh well, I knew hair grows about half-an-inch a month, so if I regretted my decision it would only take . . . *two years* to grow back. Closing my eyes and hearing the scissors cut through my hair, I felt liberated, like a Flapper in the 1920s; like my grandmother must have felt when she sold her knee-length hair to Max Factor in World War I. Look what she did: she came to a whole new continent to make a life for herself. I might not be physically breaking from my past but I could at least shed my surfer girl image and become Mod.

With my neck exposed, the base of my skull seemed to pick up every shimmer of air that brushed past me. I felt bare and vulnerable without my curtain of hair to hide behind. But I liked it. Indeed I looked like a Carnaby Street model. I couldn't wait to shorten my skirts and buy a pair of Go Go Boots.

On Wednesday, February 8, 1967 I was rushing from one class to the next. Someone tugged on the back of my trench coat. I turned and saw my face reflected in a pair of dark aviator sunglasses worn by Marc C.

"I dreamed of you last night," he said in a breathy, sexy voice.

Was it his hair that smelled so delicious, or a cologne? I wanted to lean closer and inhale him. I wanted to reach up and touch his glossy black hair that hung long, like a Beatle, over his brow. I wanted to run my hand over his clean, white, button-down shirt.

"I was at home, sick, when you cut your hair," he said. "Mattie called and told me. I miss your hair, but I like your neck."

I was speechless. The din of voices faded and the two of us seemed to be the only people in the hallway. The electric feeling that shot through me was the same as I'd experienced that first time I met Lenny at the Bay Theater. My heart quickened. My knees felt weak.

"I was at a Laker game last night and I had a vision of you," Marc said.

The bell rang. We were late for class. He lifted his chin to me as he turned and walked away. My feet carried me into my classroom where I collapsed into the seat next to Heidi. I held my hand out for her to see. It was shaking.

"What happened to *you?*" she said.

"I just talked to Marc C." I told her. "Or I should say, he talked to me."

Our teacher shot us a look.

"I thought he was dating Ginny," she whispered.

I just lifted my shoulders and sat back in my chair, listening to my heart pound in my ears.

The next day Marc found me at lunch and told me he and Ginny broke up. He'd had his eye on me for a long time. He even remembered the day I first wore my knee-high, black boots with my sister's olive-green and black striped poncho. He seemed fascinated with my appearance, which suited me just fine.

I liked his husky voice, penetrating black-olive eyes and smooth hands. He dressed meticulously in long sleeved shirts with the sleeves rolled up, white or khaki pants, a black belt, black loafers. He had a sophisticated ease about him. Although he was a year younger than I, and half a grade behind me, he seemed older and more sophisticated.

Once we started dating, the fact that he would not be graduating until February 1968 comforted me. It meant we could continue to see each other through summer and winter and maybe by then we'd be really serious and go to the same college, maybe even live together. Marc would provide the continuity I was missing from my life. A romance with him guaranteed a future. I was no longer bobbing on the ocean in a tiny boat. Marc was my land.

That same day, after school, my father took my year book photo. He studied previous annuals to create the exact same look—dark background, hair lights, bounce-flash. Whereas at school you got two or three poses to choose from, my father took four rolls of 2 ¼" film. I chose the picture, my dad printed it and we sent it in to the yearbook company, no one the wiser.

The next night, Marc and I talked on the phone for hours. He was smart and knowledgeable about so many things—politics, music, literature. Three years before I had fallen in love with Lenny, talking to him on the phone, and now I was falling in love with Marc the same way. But now I felt like a woman, not a girl, ready to experience adult love.

On Friday night Marc picked me up in his white, 1965 Volvo and we drove up narrow, winding Los Robles, in a woodsy part of the Palisades. We parked in a vacant lot, on a cul-de-sac above, Pacific Coast Highway. We could see ribbons of red and white car lights on the highway below, and a crescent moon shimmering on the black ocean.

Marc's Volvo had the gear shift on the steering column, so when we made out there was nothing between us. My Ma Griffe perfume, Marc's clean hair, car leather, eucalyptus and salt air was an intoxicating blend. On the radio Herman's Hermits sang, *There's a kind of hush all over the world tonight, all over the world people just like us are falling in love.*

I was falling in love. My worries faded away as we kissed. I felt safe.

Saturday night Marc took me to see *Dear John*, a Swedish film. The soundtrack introduced me to Mozart whose music perfectly expressed the love a dark-haired soldier, who looked so much like Marc, felt for the blond heroine, who looked a little like me, before I cut my hair. Mozart's 21st Piano Concerto became "our song."

The next Wednesday, my parents went out of town to give a lecture. They would be gone two-weeks. They hired Fay, a seventy-something grandmother who lived on Latimer Road, to stay with me. She was quiet and stayed to herself. But every night she cooked. I remember the succulent stuffed pork chops that filled our modern house with a comforting, old-fashioned almost farm-kitchen aroma.

On Friday, Marc and I hung out together after school. We lay on the lawn of the Santa Monica Civic Auditorium, gazing into each other's eyes. Van Morrison's "Brown Eyed Girl" came out that spring. Whenever I hear "behind the stadium with you . . . my brown-eyed girl," I think of Marc, on that lawn, my brown-eyed boy.

We went out to dinner, I don't remember where. But that night we decided that he would spend the night with me.

MIDNIGHT MOONLIGHT

We kissed at the door.
I came inside, brushed my teeth,
turned out the lights and
went to bed.
Marc drove his Volvo
up the street. He parked
and quietly walked back
across the wooden bridge.
Did he stop to listen
to the water flowing
did he stop to listen
to the symphony of frogs?

I didn't hear the bamboo rustle
as he opened the gate
but I heard the door slide open
saw his silhouette in the moonlight
saw him move smoothly toward me.

Breathless with anticipation
I lifted the sheet
and he slid in beside me.
Right that minute
my life changed.

I surrendered to sex,
my father's religion.
I was his daughter after all
his blood was
my blood.

I thought, *now I understand my father,*
now I know what life is for.

I was freed from despair
by wonderful kisses
I was filled up with light
empowered, transformed.

The miserable child
was burned up in passion
that midnight
in the moonlight
that weekend
she died.

In the morning Marc got dressed and slipped out the sliding glass door. I languished in my newfound contentment. A few minutes later the doorbell rang. I put on my green quilted robe and met Marc at the front door. Faye came out of my parents' bedroom, looking a little groggy.

"It's okay, Faye, it's just Marc, he's come for breakfast."

"Oh, how lovely!" she said, "Let me get dressed and I'll cook you some eggs." When she went back into the bedroom Marc and I stared into each other's eyes. He put his arms around my waist and pulled me to him. He mussed my hair.

"I still can't get used to it being gone," he said, then he bit my neck. He waited in the living room while I got dressed. By the time I was ready, face washed, mascara heavily applied, Faye was in the kitchen.

I sat at the head of the table, my father's place and Marc sat at the foot of the table, my mother's. I felt like a queen, looking down the table at my knight, being waited on by my cook.

"I want to tell you why I broke up with Ginny," Marc said. I wasn't sure I wanted to know, but he continued. "You know her mother killed herself." I nodded. "Ginny completely freaked out. I couldn't take it. I didn't feel like I was helping her. I felt like she was pulling me down into her misery." He dipped his toast into his egg yolk.

"I watched you at school. You were like a running hose in a bucket of soapy water. Just being around you makes me feel alive."

I felt sorry for Ginny and sad that he couldn't make her happy. But he was with me now. He was helping me deal with my family problems. My future, for at least a year, was assured. I was on solid ground again, not floundering, not drowning.

Six weeks later everything changed. Marc caught up with me at school. "I need to talk to you," he said. We walked through the underpass to the football field. "I'm going back to Ginny," he said. I immediately felt ice water in my veins and thought I'd throw up. "I was a coward to abandon her. I do love you Mary Lee, I love being with you, but it's totally selfish of me to be with you now." He hugged me tight. I tried to inhale as much of him as my lungs could hold. I walked to my car, drove home and wrote:

Little girl grown
paining
like a woman
free but alone
painting
her desires
on a whim
detached
from her past
the future's dim
unattached
and uninspired
rusty wagon wheel
by the creek
gazing and dazed
to feel
so weak
so young
and
so tired.

This would become the first poem in *Tender Bough*. A few weeks later my English teacher taught us to write sonnets. I am eternally grateful. This classic form, based on a five-stress line was the perfect vehicle for me to channel my grief at losing Marc. Here is the first sonnet I ever wrote.

> The loneliness of morning's dawning rays
> came peering through the gently parting mist
> and carved my shadow in the sand today.
> The breeze was cold but inside I was kissed
> with warmth by longing thoughts of you. I gazed
> across the bleak horizon searching
> for a sign, a hope, as I had done for days.
> and then I saw you coming toward the shore
> my breath fell short as joy within me cried
> at seeing that sweet, sad eyed smile, so well
> remembered. As I reached for you the tide
> splashed round my feet and broke the spell.
> I saw then as I dropped my empty hand
> not our—but my lone footprints in the sand.

Now that I was writing, I needed a desk. I asked my father to build me one, like he'd made for their office. But I wanted a plain top, not covered in white Formica, so I could paint designs on it. He screwed a 2' x 4' plank into the wall, and anchored it with plain chrome legs. I used acrylic paint and created three circular designs—a peace sign, a dove and a flower. On this desk I became a poet, writing the fifty poems, that two years later were published in *Tender Bough*. At the time I was writing purely for myself, to transform heartache so I would not shrivel up and die.

Chapter 16

MOTHER MOVES OUT

Poetry, music and my friends helped me get through the spring of 1967. It broke my heart that Marc went back to Ginny, but I thought he did the right thing. Her mother committing suicide was much worse than my parents getting divorced. Ginny was a sweet, pretty girl. I couldn't hate her.

On my eighteenth birthday in May, my dad took me to Sears and bought me a stereo record player. He hooked it up in my closet, on the chest of drawers he'd made, so I could fall asleep with the closet doors open, listening to Bob Dylan sing "Sad Eyed Lady of the Lowlands", which described me—Sad Eyed Lady of the Gowlands.

By now, my twenty-four-year-old sister was divorced. Ann and her four-year-old daughter Tracy lived in a tiny apartment over a garage on Ocean Avenue in Santa Monica.

One day they found an abandoned desert tortoise in a vacant lot and brought it to my parents' house. Although female, she was called Sherman. She lived for many years. In the summertime she liked to sunbathe with my mother in the back yard, nestling next to her leg. (My dad hated patio furniture. He said it ruined the look of the back yard, so they put lounge pads directly on the cement.) In winter Sherman always found the warmest spots on the radiant-heated floor. If we couldn't find her, we'd look behind the toilet in the models' dressing room.

Ann dropped Tracy off at preschool every day, on her way to work at the California Clothing Mart on Ninth and Main in downtown Los Angeles. She could buy samples of the latest fashions by Betsy Johnson, and other hip designers, at a big discount. On weekends I loved to visit my sister in that little apartment and sit with her and her friends around the wooden, telephone-wire spool that functioned as her dining table. Even then, three years before the first Earth Day, she was ecologically minded, repurposing and reusing whatever she could.

One wall was completely taken up by a huge black-and-white poster of the Rolling Stones in drag, given to her by the assistant director of *The Monkees* TV show. Ann wore the hippest clothes, listened to the coolest music and was active in the anti-war movement. Sometimes her friends would pass a joint around the table but she never let them offer it to me.

I wrote lyrics to various show tunes for the YWCA Song Banquet, and we won.

But because we were graduating, I didn't get to take the trophy home with me as I'd done the previous year. For Prom, Mother fashioned a floor-length dress from a tube of gold sequin-covered fabric. For weeks after the prom, I found sequins on the couch where my date and I had made out, after he brought me home.

One more lifeline came my way on June fifth. I, along with Kathie, her sister Marie, and our friend Janet, auditioned for another Parks and Recreation production—*Guys and Dolls*. Again Michael Lembeck would be one of the leads, so he and Kathie could be together until she went off to Emerson College in Boston.

This show was even more fun than *Babes in Arms* because the songs were so great, and we got to wear costumes. I went to a thrift store and bought a vintage 1940 dress and high heels with ankle straps. I wore the outfit in the opening number, "Fugue for Tin Horns", and the closing number "Guys and Dolls." For "Bushel and a Peck," as one of the Hot Box Dancers, we wore cut-offs and gingham shirts tied at our waists, like farm girls. I was happy rehearsals would start July fifth. We'd do six performances in August.

Grad Night came. When I told Mother my friends and I planned to stay up all night she suggested I take a nap. This meant missing the graduation ceremony but I didn't mind. I didn't want to wear the ugly black gown and stupid hat. I didn't want to sit outside for hours in the hot sun, while over 500 students listened to speeches and wound their way up on stage to get their diplomas. I was sad enough about school ending. To me the graduation ceremony seemed more like a funeral than a celebration.

In first grade, I had a crush on Scott C. who grew up to be tall and handsome, kind of a slimmer version of Elvis Presley, with thick, shiny auburn hair. Scott's father was extremely rich. His fifth wife was a famous Broadway and movie dancer. Scott and his older brother lived in a gated mansion in Beverly Hills.

When Scott and I started dating, he'd take me to that huge house with gigantic rooms full of expensive furnishings. It seemed more like a hotel. Our friends had their pick of any number of bedrooms to make out in. I never met, or indeed saw, his parents. Back in spring, when I'd told Ann that Marc and I had "gone all the way" she took me to a gynecologist way out in the San Fernando Valley and I got a prescription for birth control pills. We didn't tell my parents. It was our secret and made me feel very close to, and grateful for, my big sister.

Grad Night was held at the Coconut Grove in the Ambassador Hotel. I wore a very short, gold lamé mini dress, sparkly gold tights, gold pumps, and long golden earrings. My friend Chrissie wore a silver dress and silver tights. Finally our skirts could be a whole foot above our knees and we wouldn't get in trouble. We felt so liberated and grown up.

Most of the night is a blur. The Blossoms opened for the Righteous Brothers. We ate at round tables and danced for hours. Lots of kids snuck outside to drink, and smoke cigarettes or joints, but not me. Sex was my drug and I had plenty of it with Scott back at his father's mansion after the party.

In the morning I woke up in a tangle of sheets, Scott snoring loudly. My gold dress and shoes, his pants and shirt were on the floor. I stumbled out of bed and into the famous dancer's mirror-lined bathroom—walls *and* ceiling. I bent to drink from the enormous sink, turned the golden faucet and splashed water on my face. My eyes were puffy, my hair matted, my mouth tasted terrible.

I pulled on my gold pantyhose and slipped my rumpled dress over my head, then snuck quietly out of the bedroom.

So, school was truly over. This was the beginning of my new life. I went into the restaurant-sized kitchen and found a black maid in a white uniform drinking coffee.

"Good mornin'" she said. I wanted to cry. She got up from the table. "You look like you could use a glass of orange juice," she said, opening the stainless steel refrigerator.

Somehow sitting with her, drinking juice, looking out over the tree lined yard, gave me hope that there would be new people in my life who would be kind to me.

Scott soon rented an apartment on Pacific Coast Highway in Malibu and was my boyfriend until he went to Hawaii later in the summer. My parents traveled a lot, both for work and separately: my father to be with his German stewardess, and my mother took classes and trips with her women friends.

One morning my father and I got into an argument. He never liked confrontation so when he started to leave the kitchen. I shouted, "Why are you so selfish? Don't you know how much you hurt other people?"

He stood with his hand on the front door knob and said, "When you're in love, nothing else matters," and left.

All I could think was *I hate you*. I knew how great sex was, how it could completely transport you to another world of infinite pleasure. It had been incredible with Marc, who I felt connected to physically, and spiritually. I respected Marc because the pain he caused me was from his decision to do the *right* thing—go back to Ginny. In my father's case, he had been doing the *wrong* thing, "having his cake and eating it too"—dishonoring his marriage vows, carrying on in public, humiliating my mother, making her worry, making her cry.

I suppose part of me was angry that my mother had put up with him for all these years, but I did see her point, if she left him she'd lose everything. What I needed to do was find out who *I* was, what *I* wanted to do, so I could move out and move on with my life.

But I didn't want to leave my home. I loved my big black cat and the constant sound and smell of the creek. I loved the shady canyon. I couldn't imagine living in an apartment. I like privacy. I could not imagine living in a dorm or having a roommate. I hated thinking about it.

At this turbulent time in my life, spiritual solace came from an unlikely source, Joe Gray, Dean Martin's double, the stunt man, who, when we were in Europe wired DON'T MAKE A MOVE TILL YOU HEAR FROM ME. Joe Gray had become friends with writer Henry Miller who turned him on to thousands of books. In Miller's book *My Bike & Other Friends*, Volume II he says:

> There was a serious side to Joe, the eternal student, you might say. Books enthralled him, probably because he neglected them for so long . . . Strange indeed to hear him talk about Marcel Proust or James Joyce in his jive language . . . Often on returning a book he had borrowed he would slap the book down and exclaim, "That's one hell of a good book, you know that?"

Joe Gray gave me *Siddhartha*, by Hermann Hesse, for my eighteenth birthday. The story resonated with me. Siddhartha was born an Indian prince. He lived a sheltered life (like I had) until one day he ventured outside the walls of his palace and saw all the suffering of the world—illness, death, injustice. He left his home on a quest to find the meaning of life. Sitting under the *Boddhi* Tree, observing that life is like a river, and that all souls are on the same journey, he experienced enlightenment and became known as the Buddha.

My "river of life" was the ocean, my *Bodhi* tree the wall at State Beach. I wrote this sonnet one foggy day when the beach was empty:

> I sat alone in contemplation on
> the cold deserted beach. The gray of sky
> and ocean, sand and I were one. High
> up in the sky a white gull glided on
> translucent currents downward toward the calm
> quiet, peaceful swells. The purity of such
> white grace upon the toneless-ness was much
> like reassuring me that all my qualms
> and fears of truly being alone were
> so wrong. And just when I began to feel
> the grainy smoothness in my hands and peel
> the dullness from inside, I felt the stir
> of wind blow through the fog and felt the sun
> within and all around. Yes, we are one.

Joe Gray also gave me Freud's *Interpretation of Dreams.* I read it the summer between high school and the rest of my life. Because Freud placed so much emphasis on our sexual impulses, it reverberated with me—my dad's womanizing, and my own sexual awakening.

These two books opened my mind to other ways of looking at life. They helped me put my own longings, desires and suffering in a bigger context. They connected me to the greater world, if not yet physically, then at least mentally.

I recently found a letter from Henry Miller, dated April 23, 1972. In it he talks about Joe who passed away in 1971.

I always remember you as I saw you with Joe Gray. His
death was a blow to everyone, and to me more than to
any one, I do believe. He was a true friend, something
rare in this fucked up world of ours. Sure artists are
different—another species entirely. Go wherever your
heart bids you go—not just to Paris, but everywhere!
Cheers and thanks again for your poems!! Henry

In July, Mother rented an apartment across the street from Ted's
Grill and told my father he had to move out. As before, he refused.
So this time she moved.

She put a foam pad on a door supported by cinder blocks. The
kitchenette had a counter. She took two stools from home. That
was it for furniture. She installed a phone. Every morning she came
to the house to work, and at the end of the day she returned to the
apartment. I suspect most nights she spent with Jo or one of her
other friends.

Thank goodness I had *Guys and Dolls* to distract me from my
parents' troubles.

It was thrilling to be part of a cast and know we'd be performing
such a fun show. Besides parks and high school auditoriums, we
did a performace at the Santa Monica Civic Auditorium. It was
fantastic, with Craig Safan again as musical director. The show was
a big hit. I loved every minute of it.

Josh, the artist, was home from college for the summer, so we
went out a lot. Marc called from time to time. I loved his voice and
talking to him on the phone. Ginny was going off to college soon.
Reading about reincarnation, I figured he and I must have been
together in a past life, and because there was still desire, that we
would be together again in the future. I just needed to be patient.

Reasoning means nothing
all logic is absurd
you are the love of my life
the magic, echoing word

The last week of August held the highest and lowest points of my life, so far. Monday I felt sick, so I missed rehearsal at the Santa Monica Civic. But by Tuesday I made it for the show, which was spectacular. The auditorium was almost full. The acoustics were great as our voices rang out, filling the auditorium with those memorable songs, "Sit Down You're Rocking the Boat", "If I were a Bell," "Bushel and a Peck" with me as one of the Hot Box dancers, and the resounding closing "Guys and Dolls" with the entire cast filling the stage.

Wednesday we rehearsed at Beverly High School, a smaller, more intimate venue and did a great performance there on Thursday night. Josh came to the show and afterwards the two of us shared English Muffins at Ships Restaurant in Westwood. I felt like a star.

But at home I was miserable. I didn't like being in the big house alone with my father, hearing him talk to his mistress on the phone, or see him get all spiffed up for a date. Finally I couldn't stand it anymore. That Friday I decided to move in with Mother.

It was strange leaving the performance. I drove west on Sunset Boulevard but instead of taking the Brooktree Road turnoff, I continued down Chatauqua to the beach. I parked on Mesa Road. When I got out of my car, I heard laughter coming from people leaving Casa Mia, our favorite Mexican restaurant, and the Friendship gay bar. It was a beautiful, warm August night. I could smell the ocean. When the signals turned red and traffic stopped for a minute, you could hear waves breaking. Then the lights turned green and off everyone went, speeding north to Malibu and south to Palos Verdes.

I found Mother lying on her makeshift bed, reading.

"How'd it go?" she asked.

I sat beside her and told her all about the show performance.

"Peter brought down your bed," she said. Sure enough he had neatly piled my pillow, sheets and blankets on top of the box spring and mattress on the floor. In the small bathroom I brushed my teeth, washed my face and rubbed Moon Drops lotion into my face wondering where my cat was sleeping tonight.

"Goodnight," I called to Mother as I closed the bedroom door. I was too tired to sleep. I just laid there listening to cars and strangers voices, and watching head lights that flimsy curtains didn't keep out, move across the wall.

The next night was our last show. Closing Night. End of an era. The performance was great. When I got to the beach, I parked my car on Mesa Road and walked down to State Beach to mingle with some of the cast members. Not many people were there. Some guys had brought beer. I didn't see Kathie and Michael. They were probably making out back at Lembeck's house in Beverly Hills or somewhere up on the bluffs overlooking the ocean. I didn't stay long. The whole gathering was so sad. I said goodbye to the few friends I'd miss and carried my sandals as I walked barefoot back up the beach.

In the parking lot I dusted off my feet and put on my sandals. The pee-scented underpass reminded me of a dimly lit train tunnel. I emerged on the other side of the highway and walked the half-block back to the apartment.

When I opened the door, Mother was quietly talking on the phone. I went straight to the bathroom. I had a bad feeling, seeing how she was curled up cradling the phone, so lovingly.

"I'm going home," was all she said. And she meant now. I was too angry, tired, sad and confused to respond. I probably said, "fine" and closed the bedroom door.

Monday I started looking for a job. On Thursday Kathie flew to Boston to begin school at Emerson College. I went to the house almost every day, to visit my cat, get a change of clothes, check to see if I had any messages. Mother had paid the apartment rent through September. I hoped to earn enough to be able to pay October's rent myself. I was determined to be free of my parents and take control of my own life.

And then a wonderful thing happened: Marc called. I had my period and bad cramps, so I just curled up with a hot water bottle and talked to him on the phone for hours.

That Friday I had dinner with my parents. My father said he'd talked to Bob Crosby, Bing Crosby's brother, who he knew somehow.

Bob would see that I was allowed to join the Extras Union. My dad was willing to pay the $200.00 dues. I thanked him, even though being an extra and just standing around all day didn't sound very interesting. Minimum wage in 1967 was $1.65 an hour. Extras got $35.00 a day, plus lunch. It sounded pretty boring but maybe it would lead to something else.

That Saturday I landed a job in the hosiery department at C.H. Baker Shoes in Beverly Hills. I took it, figuring two job opportunities were better than none. I didn't mind working Saturdays because then I'd have a weekday available for Extra work.

With my first paycheck I bought a pair of knee-high off-white, vinyl Go-Go Boots and a purse made of brown wooden beads. I loved having my own money for the first time in my life.

I worked two weeks and then came down with strep throat. Mother drove me to my childhood doctor at the Ross Loos Medical Group on Wilshire Boulevard. I don't remember the doctor's name, only his shiny black hair, like Marc's. I was glad he couldn't read my mind because suddenly this man who had been taking care of me since I was a child seemed very handsome, with his pale forearms covered with dark hair.

As we left the doctor's office Mother said, "Come home." She got no argument from me. I missed the canyon, my room, my cat. I slept for two days and was back at work on Thursday.

Chapter 17

MARC, MARIJUANA & MOVIES

Marc had been a half-year behind me in school, but went to summer school so he could get his diploma and start college that fall. Now he attended Cal State Northridge and lived in a dorm. Even after he went back to Ginny, Marc called me every so often. He was a good listener and didn't seem to mind when I complained about my parents or expressed ambivalence about what I should do next.

The Friday after I moved home, he called and asked me to come see him. I had never driven on the freeway before. I was excited and nervous as I dressed for our date.

I turned a four-year-old baby-blue and grey pleated wool skirt into a mini-skirt by shortening it eight inches. I wore it with my new off-white go-go boots and a beige wool sweater. Underneath: red lace bra and panties. My hair was recently bleached and trimmed. If I were four inches taller, I could be Twiggy's twin.

I had to keep taking deep breaths as I drove my little Volkswagen bug—which Kathie said was like driving a roller skate (and she meant the metal kind that strapped onto your shoes) all the way out to Northridge, *at night*. My heart raced as I looked for signs for the college, then the dorm.

When I entered the brightly lit lounge, I saw students playing pool and sprawling on beat-up couches. I heard Donovan's "Mellow Yellow" coming from a juke box and noticed posters announcing an upcoming anti-war protest.

Suddenly I felt Marc's hot breath of my neck. This took me right back to that first day he grabbed me, six months before, at Pali High. I turned, expecting to see my darling black-haired boy with a Beatles haircut in a crisp white shirt. I nearly fell over when I saw a man with a beard and shoulder-length hair, wearing a green flannel shirt and blue jeans. Marc had become a hippie, right down to his suede moccasins.

He embraced me. I closed my eyes. He smelled the same. He felt the same. I let him squeeze me, feeling the marrow in my bones melt in a warm fluid rush of love.

Marc pulled me out the door and we walked through the crisp fall night and found a secluded spot on a lawn near the football stadium. To this day whenever I hear Van Morrison sing "Behind the stadium with you, my brown-eyed girl," I think of Marc, my brown-eyed boy, holding me behind the stadium. My heart, at last at peace, slowed as he held me and kissed me and we breathed each other's breath.

On October tenth, I went to the Santa Monica Civic Auditorium with my friend Chrissie, to hear Maharishi Mahesh Yogi. Chrissie and I had been friends since our first year at Paul Revere Junior High. Her family lost their home in the 1961 Bel Air fire. Her parents were Polish immigrants who had survived the Nazis and the Communists. Her mother was Olga, the iconic lingerie designer and her father Jan, ran the business. But unlike me, whose parents worked at home, Chrissie's parents went off to work every day and

Jean, their black maid, was the person she seemed closest to. Their home was full of ornate antique furniture, quite formal. I only ever saw Olga in elegant dresses, stockings, expensive jewelry and Chrissie's father in a suit.

Besides Chrissie and I both having creative, professional parents who owned their own businesses, she and I shared a love of "pondering" which we still share to this day. We liked to philosophize and think about the mysteries of life. So, when we heard that "the Beatles guru" was going to be at the Santa Monica Civic, we just had to go.

What a sweet little man he was, like a merry elf, giggly, self-effacing, almost child-like. He seemed amused by everything—such a contrast to the serious audience who hung on his every word.

That Friday, October 13, I went to my doctor and got my ears pierced. Back then it was still considered a medical procedure. The following weekend, with my new pearl-stud earrings in place, I drove up to visit Heidi at UCSB.

She shared her dorm room Arlene, my ex-boyfriend Lenny's sister, who popped in briefly to let us know she'd be gone all weekend and I was welcome to sleep in her bed. I tried to imagine what it would be like to have a roommate and live in a dorm, and not have my cat.

Heidi opened a draw and pulled out a little box. She had a twinkle in her eye. Was she going to ask me to try to smoke a cigarette again, just as she'd done a few years before? No, she sat next to me on the bed and opened her palm. *A joint!* We both opened our eyes wide. At last! I'd been waiting so long.

"Where'd you get it?" I asked.

"From Arlene. She said it's really strong, we should go easy."

Heidi stuffed a towel under the door and also in the bathroom where we huddled side-by-side on the rim of the tub.

"You go first," I told her. She held the joint in her hand and I struck a match. She touched the end of the joint to the flame and then put it up to her mouth, inhaling. I watched, fascinated, as she held her breath, then let out a long funnel of smoke and passed the joint to me.

I took it between my fingers, put up to my mouth and took a little puff.

"More," Heidi said. I inhaled a little more, tasting a mixture of herbs and flowers. As I held my breath I could feel my pulse in my ears and then involuntarily I let out a big column of smoke and began to cough.

I passed the joint back to Heidi who took another hit. Then she passed it back to me. This time I took less smoke, more air and paused to feel my lungs tingle. As I let out a controlled stream of smoke I felt my whole body relax. I noticed how light filtering in through a window made rainbows on the wall. In fact, the more I looked, little rims of rainbows were lining the sink, the tub . . . *beautiful!*

"I think that's enough for now," I told Heidi and she agreed. She snubbed out the joint, returned it to the box and we just sat for a moment looking at the way light filled the bathroom.

"My mouth is dry," I told Heidi.

"Mine too," she said, "want some Tang?"

"Sure." We left the bathroom and she mixed us two glasses of Tang. How marvelous, that scientists could capture the sweet, succulent taste of oranges, and how amazing that the taste buds on my tongue knew how to translate what was nothing but chemical formulas into such a delightful taste experience! My tongue, throat and yes, even my stomach greeted and welcomed the Vitamin C laden liquid. I could feel my stomach filling up, expanding, absorbing. What a magnificent creation—the human body!

"Why are you smiling?" Heidi asked.

"Oh," I said, opening my eyes. "I don't know," and both of us burst out in giggles.

We took the elevator down to the basement and bought snacks at a vending machines. We got back into the elevator and Heidi pushed the button for the ground floor. I tore open my bag of Corn Nuts, and popped one in my mouth. When I bit down it sounded like an explosion.

"Whoa!" I cried.

"What's wrong" Heidi asked.

"You didn't hear that?"

"No, what?" she said. Ah, good. So it was only in *my* head.

Thus, I began to learn the effects on marijuana—how my senses were amplified—touch, taste, smell, sight and sound.

During the week Marc called and asked me to come see him on the weekend. He'd be house-sitting. We'd be alone. I dressed completely differently this time.

In June I had gone to my first Love In at Griffith Park with Heidi and Joanne. Like tourists in a foreign land, we meandered through the throng of hippies, marveling at the lack of self-consciousness, the creativity in dress and the spontaneous eruptions of music and dance. Exotic fragrances filled the air—sandalwood, patchouli, marijuana. Little children and dogs romped and ran around. People played recorders and jangled tambourines. Someone blew huge bubbles. Someone else flew a kite. I dug it. I wanted to dress like the girls in colorful gypsy skirts, scarves, beads and bangles.

So I went to Europa, a big, old, warehouse-style, home-goods store with worn wooden floors, on the corner of Wilshire and Third. I bought an off-white lace tablecloth. I cut a hole in the middle and wore it like a poncho. *Voila!* Mary Lee, Flower Child.

I wasn't brave enough to wear my lace poncho with nothing underneath, so I put on a red leotard, then the table cloth, for my date with Marc. I met him at a house with a fireplace. He had built a fire. It didn't take long for the table cloth, the leotard, my bra and panties to be scattered on the floor as we made love in front of the crackling fire. Marc's clean, shiny, long black hair danced with yellow and orange light as I ran my fingers through it. The wonderful scent of burning wood, his skin, his hair, was intoxicating, better than alcohol or marijuana. The way he touched me made every cell of my body dance.

The next weekend I went back up to Santa Barbara. Heidi, Joanne and I had tickets to see the Doors. I couldn't wait to hear

"Light My Fire" in person. On the album it's nine-minutes long. How long would it go on in person?

Heidi, Joanne and I crowded into Heidi's dorm bathroom and we smoked a joint.

Then we joined the throng of students waiting to get into the auditorium.

"We're milling," Heidi said.

"Milling!" I echoed. "Come Joanne, let us mill!" Heidi and I thought this was so funny and laughed so hard tears ran down our cheeks. Suddenly Joanne clutched my arm.

"I can't see!" she cried. Heidi and I stared into her face. "I'm blind!" Joanne insisted. Could a couple hits of pot take away her sight?

"Hold on to me, Jo!" I told her, clamping her hand on my wrist. For good measure I hung on to Heidi and together we wove our way into the theater. After a few minutes Joanne regained her sight. The three of us stood and swayed with the crowd. Jim Morrison was so sexy! The guitar riffs were hot. I let myself merge with the music and the undulating light show. I felt like I was riding a never-ending wave of colors and musical notes.

On days I wasn't scheduled to work at C.H. Baker Shoes in Beverly Hills, I'd call the Extras Guild to see if they had any work for me.

I got a call to audition for a role in an upcoming MGM film. I was told to bring a bathing suit and report at 7:00 a.m. The huge sound stage, containing a swimming pool, potted palms and the façade of a house, was brightly lit with glaring flood lights that mimicked harsh summer sun.

The dozen other girls and I changed in a dressing room. I wore the bikini my parents had brought me from France two years before—red and white with an underwire bra. I could tell by the looks the other girls gave me that they'd never seen anything like it. Most of the other girls wore modest two-piece bathing suits that came up to their waists. Some even wore frumpy one-pieces.

We were directed to stand in a line in front of the pool. The director, assistant director, writer, camera man, script girl and who knows who else, sat in tall director's chairs with clipboards. We stood facing them with bright lights in our eyes, so we could not see their faces. A disembodied voice told us to turn, then turn again, so they could see all sides of us. I felt a shiver and wanted to bolt out of there. This was nothing like being in the Miss Palisades pageant where we got to smile and wave to the crowd. This wasn't like posing for my father either, because he knew how to banter and make his models laugh. He knew how to make people feel comfortable. This was so cold and impersonal, almost clinical.

A man's voice intoned, "If we call your name, thank you for coming, you may go." I felt like I might vomit.

One by one, girls' names were called and they left the soundstage. Finally there were four of us left. The bright lights dimmed and we could see the faces of the crew.

"Congratulations," a woman said. "Please report back tomorrow at 7:00. There will be two or three days work. Bring the bathing suits you're wearing and any other things you'd wear around a pool, such as straw hat, sunglasses, cover-up."

We started to head back to the dressing room. Two of the girls hugged each other and began chattering. I smiled at a tall brunette who said, "This is my first movie. I'm so excited!"

I didn't want to burst her bubble so I just nodded and told her I had to run to the restroom. I put cold water on my face and took deep breaths. There was no way I was coming back here tomorrow. Anxiety increased as I drove home. I had that sick, *I don't want to go to school* feeling I had in first grade. I decided not to tell my parents. My father might carry me back to the studio, kicking and screaming.

When my dad asked me how the day went, I told him there were a lot of girls and I needed to call in, in the morning, to find out if I was wanted back. Oh, what a stupid thing to say! I should have said that I wasn't chosen. He'd never know.

Panic increased and I didn't sleep all night. At 6:00 I called in and with my best pretend-hoarse voice said I was sick and wouldn't be able to work. Then I paced around my room. I couldn't face my parents. I had to get out of the house. I decided to walk up to the park, the sun hadn't come up yet and it was eerily dim in the canyon. I didn't care. I needed air.

I walked up the dark street to Rustic Canyon Park where street lights cast long shadows through the eucalyptus trees, increasing my agitation. I kept walking. I walked down to State Beach as the sun was rising, making the waves dance with color. Then I walked up the stairs to Ocean Avenue and as long as I'd gone this far, I walked to Ann's apartment.

She was just getting up, feeding Tracy, getting ready for work. I broke down and cried, "I don't want to be an extra!" She gave me a glass of orange juice and told me to calm down.

"You're going to have to tell Peter and Mother how you feel," Ann said.

My sister had always referred to my father as Peter, maybe because she was so young (two to four years old) when he was stationed in Germany after the war? I had always called him Daddy but now I started calling him Peter too. It made me feel more equal to him, more grown up.

When Ann went to work I called home and told my father the truth. I told him I couldn't be in that movie, wearing a bikini and didn't know if I wanted to be in *any* movies. He was furious, all right.

"I knocked myself out pulling strings to get you in the union. This can lead to speaking parts and more money. What else are you going to do with your life? Work for $1.65 an hour? I'm disgusted with you," he said and hung up on me.

Eventually I had to go back home. That week my dad went to Palm Springs with his mistress, and Mother went up to San Francisco with one of her friends. I had the house to myself. I was eighteen now, no need for a babysitter. Marc came over and stayed with me. When I poured my heart out to him he said, "You should just move out."

This just made me angry. "Oh shut up!" I snapped. "Don't tell me what to do. You're not my father."

One night Heidi came over. We smoked some pot. I remember finding her standing with my closet doors open, leaning in to the stereo, listening to The Bee Gees "New York Mining Disaster 1941." We took turns standing right in front of the speakers so that our entire being was nothing but sound. We made tea with honey and were amazed how delicious it tasted. Then Mother showed up.

"What's that smell?" she asked.

"Pot!" I said happily, never thinking she'd mind. After all she was a left-wing anti-war Democrat.

"I don't want that in my house," she said and that old anger I remembered so well, from our years of screaming at each other, emerged. "It's illegal. When you have your own home and pay your own rent you can do what you want, but as long as you're living under my roof, you live by my rules!"

What a downer! She might just as well have thrown a bucket of cold water on us. I walked Heidi out to her car. She was staying at her parents only a mile away.

"I didn't think your mom would like it!" she said as she got in her car.

Not long after that I told my mother I would be spending the night with Marc. When I returned the next day I found my birth control pills sitting on the bathroom sink. I kept them in an orange-and-yellow clutch purse Jo Lathwood had given Mother (which I still have) that I'd appropriated. Evidently Mother had come looking for it.

Mother was pretty matter of fact when she told me, "If you're old enough to have sex and smoke pot, you're old enough to support yourself. You can do whatever you want in your own home. But you obviously can't live by my rules, so it's time you move out. Little bird fly out of the nest!"

"Where am I supposed to go?" I cried, following her into the kitchen.

"You need to start saving your money and find an apartment, like any other adult," she said. "As Kahlil Gibran wrote, *Your children are not your children, they come through you but not of you.*"

I couldn't imagine feeling any worse—being kicked out of my home! The fact that all my friends wanted to be independent didn't make me feel any better. What was wrong with me?

Mother must have seen the misery on my face because she said, more calmly, "Look, I tell you what. I'll pay your rent, if you enroll in school. Work part time, go to school part time."

Winter semester at Santa Monica City College started in six-weeks. I'd need to find a roommate. I called Chrissie, who was still living at home, attending Pierce Community College in the San Fernando Valley.

"How'd you feel about living together?" I asked.

Chapter 18

TOPANGA

It took several months for things to come together. I needed a better job, where I could make more money. My car was paid for and Mother said she'd pay my rent if I went to school, so I'd need to earn enough to cover food, gas, clothes, records, utilities and car insurance. Ann found me my next job at the California Clothing Mart, where she worked, on Ninth and Main Streets in downtown Los Angeles.

Fred and Lisa Gruner were a middle aged Jewish German couple. I don't know how they got out of Germany before the Nazis took over. They never discussed it. They represented a hip new clothing line called Charlie's Girls. Their showroom was a long skinny room with three buyer's tables along one wall and clothing racks on the other. My job was to model the clothes, type sales orders and invoices, make coffee and answer the phone. I changed clothes in a tiny space behind my desk, and every morning Lisa had me wipe the telephone receiver with cotton dipped in perfume.

Lisa later told me she judged people by the condition of their fingernails. She was outgoing, diligent and fastidious. Buyers loved her. Her husband, Fred, seemed bored. Sometimes he'd stand in the doorway and watch people walking by. If he saw a woman dressed in pink he'd shout, "Good morning Miss Pink!" But most of the time he sat at one of the buyer's tables and read the L.A. Times.

I started work the first week in January, 1968. When the new semester started in February, the arrangement was for me to work three days a week and go to school two days.

After my first week, I got to work "Market Week" at the Biltmore Hotel. I slept at the Gruner's house the Sunday night before and was surprised in the morning when Lisa took bacon out of the freezer for Fred's breakfast. First of all, I didn't know you could freeze bacon, and second, I thought Jews didn't eat pork. I guess they weren't very religious.

Working at the Biltmore was a blast. Many more buyers came to our hotel room and I got to change in a nice big bathroom. The Gruners went home after a long day and let me spend the night in the comfortable hotel room. The first night I ever spent alone! I felt very grown up.

The poem, "Second Story Warehouse" by Edward Hirsch, inspired me to write about working for the Gruners:

CHARLIE'S GIRLS

Come with me to the eleventh floor
of the California Clothing Mart
on Ninth and Main, in downtown
Los Angeles where I worked in 1968.

Follow me down the hall to the showroom
of Fred and Lisa Gruner, husband and wife,
holocaust survivors, who worked side by side
in "the rag trade" for over twenty years.

Let me point out the long closet on the left
and the three partitioned tables on the right
where buyers sat and watched me model
mini skirts and fitted knits by *Charlie's Girls*.

Let me take you into the narrow space where
I changed clothes, made coffee and
dipped cotton in perfume to rub on the phone
because Lisa needed it clean and sweet.

See the desk on the right with the heavy
gray Remington on which I typed orders
and wrote a scathing letter to my father
one day when the Gruners were out,

a letter I wish I'd kept because I don't
remember the words, just my righteous anger.
He'd fallen in love with German *fräulein*.
I smacked the keys till my fingers stung.

At lunch I'd take the elevator down to the lobby,
buy a liverwurst sandwich on Russian rye,
a can of V-8, barbecue potato chips and a glazed donut
from a cheerful *spade* who liked my legs.

On April 4th Martin Luther King was killed.
Fred said, "What did that nigger ever do for you?"
I went into the white-tiled bathroom and
cried so hard I threw up. Even though

I loved Lisa like a mother I had to quit.
I couldn't believe someone who suffered so much
could be so cruel. I went to work at the Sheffield
Watch Company where I was alone all day. My boss

was a traveling salesman. I tagged broken watches and
studied astrology, till Tom and I moved to Mount Shasta.

Martin Luther King, Jr. was killed in April 1968. I met Tom in October. So, let me backtrack:

In February, I enrolled at Santa Monica City College, selecting courses that met Tuesdays and Thursdays. On Mondays, Wednesdays and Fridays I'd meet my sister at her apartment on Ocean Avenue and together we'd drive downtown in her white Volkswagen, dropping Tracy (age five) off at pre-school on the way. I loved when we picked up Tracy, she'd chatter away in the back seat. Her favorite lunch was cottage cheese, bacon and corn.

Marc moved out of the dorms into a house he rented with some other guys. One of them, nicknamed Rex, was super smart, and seemed much older than his eighteen years, with thinning hair and wire-rimmed glasses that contrasted with his buff, tan surfer physique. Rex was a true dichotomy—sexy, smart, absent minded. He often seemed to be in a world of his own.

I made more trips by myself up to UCSB to visit Heidi. We saw Jimi Hendrix—one of the most amazing experiences of my life. What a cool dude! Afro, wild clothes, screaming hot guitar, and English to boot! We saw Big Brother and the Holding Company with Janis Joplin. They blew our minds. We saw Cream and fell in love with Eric Clapton. I got a huge crush on the folk singer Tim Buckley and bought his album which I listened to over and over.

In March Mother rented my father an apartment in Pacific Palisades and told him she would continue to work with him but if he was in love with someone else, then he could sleep somewhere else. I think he actually tried staying in the apartment, but eventually refused, again, to move out.

Ann made a trip to San Francisco and fell in love with the city. When she returned she said she was going to move, which she did the following year and she's been there ever since.

For my father's fifty-second birthday, on April 3, 1968, my parents went out to dinner with their best friends, Jo and Benjie, and Chris and Don. Christopher Isherwood was a well-known English writer, who, when he was in his fifties, fell in love with an eighteen-year-old American, Don Bachardy. Chris, with his thick

English accent and even thicker eyebrows, was witty and wry. His best-know book, *Berlin Stories* about an English tutor in Germany before WWII was based on his own life. It became the Broadway play *I Am a Camera* and was later adapted into the musical *Cabaret*. Don became a successful, well-know portrait artist who painted or drew many famous writers, actors, politicians. I'm honored that he drew my portrait in 1965 and another in 1967. Mother, Ann and I sat for him, but I don't believe my dad ever did.

Chris and Don were the first gay couple I knew. Their deep love and respect for each other was the basis of a wonderful 2007 documentary *Chris and Don, a Love Story*. When I saw it not long ago, it brought back happy memories of my parents' talented friends.

That night, knowing I had the house to myself, I invited Marc over. Up until now I'd smoked pot with my girlfriends, but not with him. When I heard his Volvo drive up, I went outside to greet him.

We hugged and kissed. Then he reached into his pocket and brought out a joint. "We better smoke it outside," I said. "If my parents come home and smell it, they'll be pissed off."

We sat on the steps above the pool and passed the joint back and forth. Part of me wanted to stay there all night listening to the crickets and gazing at the stars. But when he kissed my neck, my attention turned to him. I followed him back inside. With my glass bedroom door open to the night sounds and smells, we made love.

But something wasn't right. I must have smoked too much. I felt dizzy and disoriented. I felt like I couldn't breathe. I got up and stood in the open doorway trying to clear my head. But when I took a deep breath of the cool canyon air I felt I was filling my lungs with sadness.

"I'm going to take a shower," I said and went into the bathroom. Marc followed.

As we stood together in that little space, with warm water rushing over us, I started to cry. All my sadness, confusion and fear poured out of me. But instead of it making me feel better, I felt like I was melting and flowing down the drain.

I turned the water off, wrapped a towel around my head and went into my bedroom. Marc sat on the bed beside me and stroked my shoulder.

"Calm down, shhhh," he said but I just couldn't stop crying. "Maybe you should call your sister," he suggested.

He stood in the kitchen with me as I dialed the phone. When Ann answered I burst into tears again.

"I'm too stoned!" I cried. Ann said to hold on. I could hear loud music in the background. A moment later, Linda, Ann's landlord's daughter, who was my age, got on the phone. I started pouring out my heart to her.

"I'll be there in five minutes," Linda said.

Marc and I got dressed. I walked him outside just as Linda's Volkswagen Bug drove up. I felt like a doctor had arrived. Linda and Marc greeted each other and Linda walked with Marc to his car. They seemed to be consulting. Then she came back and put her arm my shoulder.

"What you need is some chamomile tea," she said and steered me into the kitchen.

And thus began an intense, life-changing relationship.

This was not the first time Linda would "talk me down." Although she was only a few months older than I, she seemed like an "old soul." She had a broad face, wild strawberry-blond hair. She dressed like Janis Joplin, in colorful scarves, beads and many jangling bangles on her arms. I would soon learn that Linda believed in magic and had read the *Lord of the Rings*. Sometimes she wore a hooded cape and carried a staff. That night, after making me tea, she and I went into the back yard.

"Listen," she said. I heard the familiar gurgling creek, frogs, crickets and in the distance, the faint rolling ocean. "Now take a deep breath," she instructed. I breathed in the woodsy smells mixed with salt air. "Now look up," she pointed. "See Venus? That's your star sign. Venus rules Taurus. It's the planet of love."

"What sign are you?" I asked her.

"Aquarius, like the age we're now entering, an age of space exploration, when religion and science will mesh and humankind will fulfill our true potential."

It took three days for me to completely come down from my marijuana overdose. I called work and said I was sick. On Sunday Ann and I went to see Mel Brooks' *The Producers,* which is still one of my favorite movies.

I worked every day of spring break, saving money to move. I didn't talk to Marc for a couple of weeks. I was too embarrassed to call him and he was probably too freaked out to call me. My parents and I continued to have fights.

On April 27th I saw an ad for a house for rent on Topanga Canyon Boulevard and Pacific Coast Highway in Malibu. I called Chrissie and asked her if she'd come look at it. I remember the two of us peering into the window of the little white-shingled house next to the Malibu Feed Bin. Across two-lane Topanga Canyon Boulevard was a Gulf gas station. Across six-lane Pacific Coast Highway was Topanga Beach.

But we didn't focus on the traffic or noise. We were enchanted by this little cottage that was probably built in the 1930s.

"I bet it's $300 a month," I sighed, which was way over our budget. But it turned to out to be only $150.00 a month, $75.00 each. Affordable!

The house had a living room with a worn painted floor, a kitchen with no cabinet doors, a bathroom with tub, sink, toilet and water heater, and two small bedrooms. My bedroom had an outside door to a small wooden deck enclosed with latticework. Chrissie's room had a window that overlooked "the Snake Pit," a rustic area that included a seasonal creek and lots of sycamore trees, poison oak, sumac and other native plants similar to the canyon where I grew up.

Suddenly leaving my parents' home didn't seem so bad. Our parents signed the rental agreement. I'd move in on Wednesday, May first, but Chrissie had tests at school and wouldn't be able to move in until the weekend.

I was so excited and wanted to share my happiness. Marc didn't have a phone in that grungy house he rented with his friends, so I decided to drive out and tell him. When he wanted to call me, he used a pay phone.

Marc wasn't home, but Rex was there, sitting at the kitchen table eating a bowl of Cheerios and working on a school assignment. He was delighted to hear that I'd be living at the beach.

"I'll come stay with you, Mary Lee," he said. "I'll bring my surf board." He strapped his board on the roof of my car, and I took him home. And yes, we had sex that night, and many nights thereafter.

Being that I've always been monogamous, Rex became my summer boyfriend. I was still in love with Marc. To tell you the truth, I don't think I ever fell out of love with him. But Marc was not emotionally or physically available all the time, so Rex it would be.

Chrissie moved in on Friday, May third. The first thing she wanted to do was repaint the living room floor. We never considered sanding it first, just slapped a coat of bright green paint on it. Then, as it dried, we sat on our little stoop and watched the sun set over the ocean.

Topanga Canyon Boulevard is twelve miles of narrow hairpin turns and steep drop-offs that connects Malibu to the San Fernando Valley. Four miles inland, the village of Topanga is nestled—post office, shops, restaurants, a state park and houses scattered over the hillsides. Back in 1968 most of the houses were funky shacks—no multi-million dollar homes like there are now.

My nineteenth birthday fell on the next Monday, May sixth. I went out to dinner with my father, Ann and Tracy because Mother was in Saint John's Hospital with complications from appendicitis she's suffered when they went to Japan. I wish I could remember which of my favorite restaurants I chose: House of Lee in the Palisades, for their scrumptious fried shrimp? Casa Mia in the Canyon, for their chili rellenos? Zucky's on Wilshire, for their matzo ball soup? Or maybe we went to the Lobster on the Santa Monica pier where, when Ann was sixteen, her boyfriend drank six glasses of water.

Rex visited me once or twice a week. He'd bring his surfboard and spend all day surfing. At night I liked to cook for him. I remember cooking a turkey and eating with him at the little counter under the window in the kitchen. In the month of May I saw my favorite singer Tim Buckley at the Troubador in Hollywood, and Cream at UCSB. I went to another Love In at Griffith Park and saw The Beatle's second movie *Magical Mystery Tour*. I decorated our living room with the famous psychedelic posters of George Harrison and John Lennon. It was such an exciting time. So much was happening in music, movies, art and clothing. I started to draw, incorporating psychedelic styles and themes into my pen-and-ink drawings.

On a warm Saturday, Chrissie and I put on our bikinis and crossed the highway to Topanga Beach. Reclining against our inverted beach chairs, squinting out over the ocean, we talked about how far we'd come since the summer of 1965, when I was in love with Lenny and spent my days on this very same beach. Lenny was married now. He'd met someone at UC San Diego and settled down.

"Look at that," Chrissie said.

I shielded my eyes and peered down the shore where a scruffy-looking kid, who looked to be about twelve, was walking into the surf, fully dressed. He held a puppy in his arms. Then he bent down and put the puppy in the water. Before I realized what I was doing, I was running down the beach, shouting.

"Stop it! What are you doing?"

The boy picked up the little dog, who couldn't have weighed more than three pounds.

"I'm healing him," he said. "He has distemper."

"That's not the way to heal him. He needs to go to the vet!"

"Charlie says the ocean has healing powers."

"Come on, sit with us," I said, taking the boy's wet sleeve and pulling him out of the surf. The poor little dog's eyes were runny and it was wheezing. I led the boy back to where we were sitting. He plopped down into the sand, not caring at all that he was now wet and covered with sand.

"Where do you live?" asked Chrissie.

"I live with Charlie, in his bus," the boy responded.

"Charlie who?" Chrissie asked.

"I don't know his last name," the boy said, stroking the puppy.

"What's your name?" she asked.

181

"Paul," he said.

"How old are you?" I asked.

"Fourteen."

"Are you a runaway?" Chrissie asked.

"Yeah, I guess," he answered. "But it doesn't matter. I live with Charlie now and he takes care of me." Chrissie and I exchanged glances. "Do you want to see his bus? It's just across the street."

"Yes," Chrissie and I said together. We gathered our beach chairs and towels and stuck our feet into our *zories*.

"Come with us," I said to Little Paul—for that's what we would end up calling him, "We'll stop at our house. Has this puppy eaten today?"

"No. Neither have I."

We crossed the highway together and walked the short distance to our porch.

"Stay here," Chrissie instructed. We were both very particular about keeping sand out of our house. She and I brushed off our feet and leaned our sandy backrests against the wall.

Chrissie made Little Paul a peanut butter and jelly sandwich and I tried to get the puppy to drink milk from a bowl, but it could hardly lift its head. I poured Little Paul a glass of milk and stood over him as he ate and drank, feeling maternal toward this lost soul.

When he finished eating he led us behind our house, down into the Snake Pit.

"Don't you have any shoes?" Chrissie asked him.

"I don't like shoes. But if I need some, Charlie will get them for me."

We walked a short way along the nearly dry creek bed, then waded in the shallow water to the other side, where a big yellow school bus was parked. Little Paul pushed open the door and we followed him inside.

The bus had been gutted, all the seats removed, except for the driver's seat and the one next to it. The floors were covered in Oriental carpets. Huge silk pillows in various colors were strewn throughout. An Indian bedspread-curtain bisected the bus. Little Paul parted it and let us peer into the "inner sanctum" where a king-sized bed took up most of the space. The bed was piled with pillows and various items of clothing. Hooks attached to the sides of the bus held more clothes. All the windows were covered with fabric and the air was thick with sandalwood incense and patchouli oil.

Little Paul set the puppy down on the bed. He opened a cooler and took out a glass jar full of huge marijuana buds. "Wanna smoke?" he asked us.

Chrissie and I looked at each other. "Sure," she answered for both of us.

Little Paul tore off a bud and stuck it into the bowl of a huge red plastic bong. I had never smoked a bong before and wasn't sure how much to inhale, so I let Chrissie take the first hit and watched as the she inhaled slowly and the bong water gurgled. She held her breath for a few seconds and then let out a stream of smoke. Smiling, she passed the bong to me.

The smoke was surprisingly cool. I made sure not to take too much. I'd learned my lesson from the night I got too stoned with Marc, and never wanted to feel that out of control again. I exhaled and passed the bong to Little Paul. He took his hit and then blew the smoke directly into the puppy's nose. That poor dog. Part of me wanted to rescue it, but part of me didn't want to touch a sick animal. I really just wished the puppy would go to sleep and not wake up.

"How many people live here?" Chrissie asked.

"It changes," Little Paul said. "Right now there are . . . I think twelve of us."

"And Charlie pays for everything?" I asked.

"Yeah," Little Paul answered.

"And you don't know his last name?" I asked getting up. I saw a stack of what appeared to be unopened mail and a copy of *Life* Magazine.

"I forget," Little Paul said, taking another hit.

I casually picked up the magazine and started to leaf through it. Then I picked up one of the letters and read the name Charles Manson, a name that meant nothing to me. The address was a post office box in Hollywood.

"Well, thank you for the tour," I told Little Paul.

"Aren't you going to stay and wait for Charlie to come back? I want you to meet him."

"I want to take a shower," I answered, "I'm all salty and itchy. Maybe another time." Chrissie and I walked back to our house.

"That was a trip," she said as we waded back through the creek.

"It felt like a harem," I agreed. "But I could never live without running water."

Chrissie and I soon discovered something else we loved about our little cottage by the beach. The Gulf gas station across the street was a perfect spot for guys to hitchhike up into Topanga Canyon, or north to San Francisco. On many balmy evenings she and I set up our beach chairs and watched the action. Quite often, if a hitchhiker had been standing a long time, he'd cross the street and sit and talk to us. We'd offered juice or water, sometimes dinner. Sometimes he paid us back with weed. One time a long-haired blonde dude from Scotland gave us a knuckle sized rock of Tibetan hashish. It smelled like perfume and tasted delicious.

That night I drew into the wee hours of the morning—a detailed pencil portrait of a man and woman. I took the drawing to my art class, and got an A.

A few nights after Chrissie and I met Little Paul and heard so much about Charlie, she and were engaged in one of our favorite activities: reading to each other. This evening I was propped up in my comfy bed, and she was in hers, the doors of our rooms open. It reminded me of Mother reading me *Charlotte's Web* when I was little. Now I read from *The Prophet* by Kahlil Gibran, the 1935 edition I'd inherited from my grandmother Andy.

"'And a woman who held a babe against her bosom said, Speak to us of Children. And he said: Your children are not your children. They are the sons and daughters of Life's longing for itself. They come through you but not from you, and though they are with you yet they belong not to you.' That's the passage my mother quoted when she told me I had to move out," I said.

"Really?" Chrissie responded. "Mary Lee, that is quite profound."

"Yes, and it hurt my feelings. But now I think I understand. All of us are on our own spiritual paths. Just because we come out of a woman's physical body doesn't mean she possesses us. We all have our own destinies." I stared up at the ceiling, which I'd decorated with glow-in-the-dark stars.

"Yes, exactly!" Chrissie said. "Plus, don't forget, that the woman who is your mother in this lifetime might have been your daughter in a past life."

Just then we heard a knock and the front door opened. We never locked it when we were home. We hoped people would come in and visit us.

I sat up in bed. A shadow appeared in my doorway.

"Hey," said a man's voice.

I turned to see a man with dark curly hair and beard. He leaned against my door frame. "What's happening ladies?"

"Who are you?" I asked.

"Charlie Manson," he said, "Little Paul said to come pay you a visit."

"Well tonight is not a good time," I told him. "We're right in the middle of a very deep discussion."

"May I join you?" he asked walking into my room.

"No. This is private and personal." I told him. Then louder, "Chrissie, it's Charlie Manson. I told him we're busy."

Charlie stepped away from my door and looked into Chrissie's room.

"Oh hello, Charlie," she said. "You have a very beautiful bus. But we're engaged in a most esoteric conversation right now and don't wish to socialize. Could you perhaps come back another time?" Chrissie had a way of sounding very formal and proper, especially with strangers.

"Oh man, why are you so uptight?" he responded.

"Because we're in bed, and not in the mood to entertain," I said in a less friendly tone. "Please leave."

"Paul said you girls were very mellow but you certainly don't sound very cosmic." he answered.

"Go away!" I said in a tone I might use with a stray dog.

Finally he gave up and left.

I got out of bed and went into Chrissie's room. As always, she wore a beautiful negligee and a scented candle burned on the side table. I sat on the end of her bed in my tee-shirt and underpants.

"That was weird." I said. "I didn't get a good vibe from him at all. I don't understand why Little Paul would attach himself to someone like that."

"We're all looking for a father," Chrissie mused. "An earthly one, or a celestial one . . ."

"So," I asked, leaning back against the wall. "Who do you think your mother was in your last life?"

Saturday, June first, was cold. What they call in Southern California, "June gloom," a thick layer of fog hung along the coast, while just a few miles inland it was warm and sunny. But Chrissie and I didn't mind. We bundled up and sat in our beach chairs, watching the Gulf station across the street.

A red Chevy pulled in to get gas. From the passenger side emerged a guy in overalls, no shirt underneath, chin-length wavy brown hair, beard. He opened the back door and took out two small suitcases.

"He's cute," Chrissie said.

The hitchhiker waved to the driver, positioned himself on the sidewalk and stuck out his thumb.

"Shall we ask him if he's thirsty?" Chrissie asked. Before I could answer she called, "Yoo hoo!" and waved.

He smiled and waved back.

"Would you like a glass of water?" she yelled.

He put his hand to his ear, not hearing her over the traffic. She motioned for him to come over. He waited until there was a lull in the traffic then ran across the street.

"Hello," Chrissie said in her most gracious hostess voice. "I'm Chrissie. This is my roommate, Mary Lee. We wonder if you're thirsty, or hungry . . ."

"I'm Eric," he said, extending his hand to her. She shook it. He reached over and shook my hand. "May I use your bathroom?"

"By all means," Chrissie said. She got up and opened the door, "After you." I followed them inside.

Eric set down his suitcases. While he was in the bathroom I got him a glass of water from the sink. I looked at Chrissie and shook my head, indicating I wasn't interested. She gave me a big smile.

Eric stayed three weeks, doing—to our delight—nude yoga in Chrissie's bedroom, where he slept. Sometimes it bothered me, the sounds of their lovemaking. But I understood that she had endured many nights of me and Rex going at it. This was the price one paid for having a roommate.

Eric had hitchhiked all the way from back east and was on his way to San Francisco. The second night he spent with us, he called me into Chrissie's room, where she was lounging on the bed. He set one of his suitcases beside her and opened the two latches. It was completely filled with kilos of marijuana.

"Wow," Chrissie and I said together. Neither of us had ever seen so much dope.

"I have to sell this in San Francisco," he said, closing the suitcase, clearly happy we were so impressed. "But, I can share this." From his overall pocket he took out a lid. He opened the baggy and took a big sniff. "Maui Wowie," he said and put it under our noses. It smelled wonderful.

Eric rolled a fat joint. We sat on Chrissie's bed and smoked a couple hits. Then we all went into the living room to listen to the Beatle's *White Album.*

Tuesday, June fourth was the California Primary election. Voting age was twenty-one, so we couldn't vote yet. President Johnson, beleaguered by the Vietnam War, dropped out after he didn't do well in several primaries. My parents voted for Eugene McCarthy. Chrissie's parents, Republicans, voted for Richard Nixon.

In the early morning hours of June 5th, celebrating his victory in California, Robert Kennedy was assassinated by Sirhan Sirhan, at the Ambassador Hotel in Los Angeles, the same place we'd had our Grad Night party just a year before. What the hell was happening to our world? The poor Kennedys!

Many Democrats, my parents included, didn't think Hubert Humphrey should automatically get Robert Kennedy's delegates. They wanted a new primary in California. I joined a protest march in Century City, but it did no good. Humphrey went on to be the nominee and lost to Richard Nixon. Humphrey received 42 percent, Nixon 43.4 percent, and third party candidate George Wallace got 13.5 percent of electoral votes.

With the death of Robert Kennedy, so soon after Martin Luther King, Jr., I felt like the world was exploding, or imploding, or just completely falling apart. I was glad I hadn't brought my little black-and-white TV with me when I moved to Topanga. I didn't want to watch the nightly news reports of mounting casualties in Vietnam. I wanted to tune out the violent world and focus on what made me happy: music, sex, drugs, the ocean, drawing and writing poems.

On June twelfth Chrissie got a nose job. I thought her nose was perfectly fine but she insisted there was a little bump on the bridge she wanted fixed and it would be no big deal. When I visited her at her parents' house two days after her surgery, she looked like she'd been in a head-on collision—two black eyes and big bandage over her nose.

While Chrissie recuperated at her parents' house, I got to know Linda better. I hadn't spent much time with her since the night I got too stoned with Marc at my parents' house. She and I went to the Troubador in West Hollywood to hear a young Canadian folksinger named Joni Mitchell. We both loved her lyrics and melodies. I bought her album *Song to Seagull.* Many of the songs seemed to be about us, or people we knew.

Linda lived in a little 1930s apartment in Ocean Park. She had a puppet of Sim Sala-bim with a big pointed hat, and a little black puppy, Poppin who she nicknamed Ratty Bolognie. She'd take that dog's face in her hands and sing, "Pull your ears and make you cry . . ."

Linda seemed like a precocious child, mad scientist, and performer rolled into one. She approached life as a magical adventure, a theatrical event. One afternoon, in her apartment, we smoked some crumbly green Moroccan hash and listened to "Hey Jude." I'd heard it on the radio in my Volkswagen a hundred times. But now, in Linda's stucco apartment, I felt like I was front-row-center with celestial orchestral strings swirling around me, lifting me to the stars.

Eric stayed with me another week while Chrissie was still at her parents'. When he left, in gratitude for our hospitality he gave us several baggies of that great pot and a hardback copy of the *I Ching*. When Chrissie returned from her convalescence, she said I could keep it. I used that *I Ching* almost religiously over the next twenty years, particularly during turbulent times in San Francisco, when I was completely unmoored from my Southern California life.

Psychologist Carl Jung says in his 1949 introduction, "The *I Ching* does not offer itself with proofs and results; it does not vaunt itself, nor is it easy to approach. Like a part of nature it waits until it is discovered. It offers neither facts nor power, but for lovers of self-knowledge, of wisdom—if there be such—it seems to be the right book."

Eric also left us something we had been curious about and wanting to try: mescaline. From a baggie that must have contained hundreds of big white capsules he gave me a handful. When Chrissie returned I divided it between us. I put mine in an empty aluminum film can, tucked it into my sewing kit, and stowed it on the top shelf of my closet.

Chrissie returned with her new nose. I passed my finals at Santa Monica City College. Now that summer was here, I'd be working for the Gruners full time. I worked my second Market Week at the downtown Hilton and came home every night that week to a sunburned Rex who had spent his days surfing.

On Friday, June 28th, Chrissie called me into her bedroom. "Do you want to try the mescaline tonight? There's a free concert up in the canyon."

We knew the names of many types of psychedelics—mescaline, psilocybin, LSD, peyote, magic mushrooms—and were of the opinion that mescaline was the mildest and somehow more "natural" than the others, except for peyote and mushrooms which were reported to make you throw up.

"Okay," I said. "But should we take it here, or wait until we get up into the canyon?"

"We'll take it here, with a glass of milk just before we leave," she said. "Now let's decide what to wear." I opted for my lace table cloth, with just a bra and panties underneath. Chrissie wore hip-hugger bell bottoms with a tie-dye tank top.

We took turns in the little bathroom. My idea of painting the water heater and sink bright orange wasn't very successful. The sink was peeling something awful and the water heater smelled like burning paint whenever we ran hot water. How naive I was to think "enamel" paint meant I could paint an enamel sink.

By now the "Twiggy lashes" were out of style and a more natural look was in, so I went light on the make-up. I put on big hoop earrings made of bone, and wore my favorite blue thongs. Before we left, we swallowed the mescaline capsules. Chrissie said she'd drive.

Taj Majal, a soulful singer with a gravelly voice, performed with his band, on a flatbed truck. His first, self-titled album was released later that summer. Getting out of the car, I discovered a beautiful iridescent beetle, about four inches long. Worried that someone would smash it, I made it my mission to rescue it. I needed to find something to scoop it up with, and put it safely in the bushes. But I didn't want to wander away from the beautiful creature.

Eventually I put out my hand and it crawled into my palm. Then like a Batmobile it opened its wings and took off in flight. I watched it ascend into the night sky amazed at how much brighter the stars were up here in the mountains, away from beach fog. And how *many* stars there were. It dawned on me that the billions of stars in the sky were like the billions of atoms in my body. I was a universe unto myself, separate yet connected to the great universe. Yep, the mescaline was working.

I continued to work five days a week through July. Chrissie came down with Valley Fever, a mysterious serious bronchial infection, and stayed at her parents' house for nearly three weeks. Rex visited me a couple of days a week. He also spent time surfing at Latigo Canyon further up the highway, which was less crowded and had bigger waves. He introduced me to some of his surf buddies including a teenager we called Young Boy, YB for short.

One Saturday night I was alone when a friend from high school, Jere Collins, came by with a couple of his friends. I put on the Beatles' *White Album* and sliced some fresh peaches.

"I brought some wood rose," Jere told me.

"What is it?"

He reached into his jeans pocket and pulled out a couple of brown capsules. "It's an herbal psychedelic. Do you want to try it?"

"Is it like mescaline?"

"Kinda," he said. "But, it's a completely different plant."

"Okay," I said.

He followed me into the kitchen. I took a capsule with a glass of water. He took one too. We went back into the living room. I sat on the floor. Jere sat on our "couch," the door set on cinder blocks, with a foam pad on top, covered in an Indian bedspread that had been Mother's bed when she briefly left my dad.

In a few minutes I started to feel nauseas. I went to the bathroom and retched but didn't throw up. I sipped water from the faucet. My head felt hot. I went into my room to lie down but this made me feel dizzy. I stood up. I needed air. I went out onto my little lattice-enclosed patio. I had to hold on to the lattice work to steady myself. Suddenly I felt something wet. I looked down. I had wet my pants. I started to hiccup. I had a hard time catching my breath.

I went back into my bedroom. I stepped out of my pants and sat on the bed. I could hear the Beatles singing "*Oh bla de, Oh bla da.*" I could hear male voices and muffled laughter. The music and voices seemed to get further and further away. I could hear my heart beat. I realized I wasn't breathing. *Oh,* I thought, *I'm going to die tonight, if I don't remember to breathe. I must take a breath.*

I took a breath and felt as if I were floating out of my body. I was flat on my back, gazing up at my star-covered ceiling, and at the same time I was looking down on a nineteen-year-old girl in a white blouse and no pants. The atoms of her body began to slow. Her eyes closed. Sounds grew fainter. She wasn't remembering to breathe. She wasn't afraid, she was just aware that if she did not breathe she would die. Everything went black.

I woke up Sunday morning with a dry mouth and terrible headache. I never took wood rose again. And I never saw Jere again. He was killed in a car wreck a week later. The black Porsche he'd been given for graduation crossed the double yellow line and hit an oncoming truck head on, just a few miles north on Pacific Coast Highway. Was he drunk? Was he stoned? I never found out.

On the day Jere was killed, Sunday, July 28th, I went with my mother and sister to a protest in Century City. We still hoped that the Democratic Party would not give Robert Kennedy's delegates to Humphrey. But they did and he lost anyway.

The first Saturday in August, Linda and I took a trip down to Laguna Beach about an hour south. The small artistic town had many art galleries, book stores, and head shops that sold all sorts of pipes, bongs, tie-die clothes, candles, and incense. Little restaurants served vegetarian and Indian foods. The whole town looked beautiful, bathed in the soft ocean sunlight. It smelled good too.

We entered a cool, dim bookstore and spent a long time browsing the metaphysical and spiritual shelves. One of the clerks, a skinny young guy with hair past his shoulders, asked if we'd like to see their mandala. He led us down a hallway to an empty room with a deep blue carpet. One wall was covered with a circle-shaped mural that represented the earth, mostly in shades of blue and green.

"Make yourselves comfortable," the clerk said, closing the door behind him.

Linda and I sat cross-legged in front of the mural. At the top, very small, we could make out a human figure. The rest of the painting was teeming with sea creatures, land animals, plants, mountains, valleys.

"Here," Linda said. She held out a joint to me. I took it. From a little velvet pouch she took out a book of matches. We each took a couple hits. Then she snuffed out the joint and put it back in her velvet pouch.

I have no idea how long we stared at that painting. It might have been minutes that felt like hours, or hours that felt like minutes.

A group of high school friends and I went to Disneyland to celebrate Joanne's eighteenth birthday, on August 10th. I hated it. Hot, dry, crowded, everything fake, man-made. We shuffled along with the crowds, stood in long lines, went on a few rides and ate overpriced fast food.

On the eleventh, I had dinner with my mother's best friend Jo Lathwood, in her little upstairs apartment on Channel Road. By now Jo was living alone. She'd kicked Benjie out. They had lived together for twenty-one years but never married. Jo was thirty-five and Benjie was twenty-one when, as a young Marine just back from World War II, she met him at the Friendship Bar down the street from her apartment. She took him home with her and he stayed for two decades.

They appeared to be the perfect couple: she, an artist and sportswear designer, he a writer. Every winter they went away for three months to a tropical location—Haiti, Hawaii, Jamaica, the Bahamas—where they stayed in grass shacks or cheap hotels. Jo painted. Benjie wrote. The other nine months they were a permanent fixture on State Beach. They had many artist and writer friends. At their dinner parties everyone sat on pillows on the floor at a low, round marble table. Writers like Tennessee Williams and Christopher Isherwood were frequent guests. Actresses Julie Harris and Ann Baxter were two of Jo's closest friends. But my mother was Jo's *best* friend and vice versa.

Yes, Jo and Benjie appeared to be the perfect couple, until Benjie fell in love with one their closest friends, a woman ten years younger than him. After all, when Benjie met Jo she was a hot thirty-five year old, but now she was over sixty and he was still in his forties. For years he didn't act on his feelings. Then for a long time he and "the other woman" were discreet. But eventually the lie could not be sustained. Benjie drank heavily. The other woman wanted him to go to AA, but when he told Jo, she poo-pooed the idea. Jo liked having her rum and coke every night and didn't see anything wrong with him having a couple of drinks, too.

Finally Benjie couldn't keep his secret any more. He confessed to my father who had always been open with my mother. My father prized honesty over deceit even if it meant people got hurt. My father assured Benjie that if he came clean, Jo and he could work something out.

Benjie didn't want to leave Jo. He loved her. Maybe they could have an "open marriage." After all, this was the "Swinging Sixties" when couples sometimes had key parties. Husbands would toss their car keys into a fishbowl and the wives would close their eyes and select a set. Then the new couples paired off in different bedrooms.

Benjie saw my parents' marriage as an example of how people could stay together under "unconventional" circumstances. About this time Mother decided she and my dad should get some counseling. Dr. Rodrick Gorney had recently published a book called *The Human Agenda*. My mother and father went to see him.

After hearing their situation, Dr. Gorney asked, "Alice, do you love Peter?"

"Yes!" she replied.

"Well, he's not going to change," Dr. Gorney said. "If you want to be with him you're going to have to be the one to compromise."

I don't know how long it took my mother and father to come to an agreement but here it is: if my father came to Mother to ask for money to take out his mistress or buy her gifts, or go on trips—remember my mother handled all the money, my father never had more than a few dollars in his pocket—then she would keep track in a little ledger and for every dollar he spent, she gave herself credit. She'd let it accumulate until she had a reason to spend it. Over the next few years she took French lessons, and took trip to France. She even bought a house, with a friend of hers.

The second thing Mother wanted had to do with the anxiety of my father not coming home at night. She told him he should pick a night—he chose Monday—and that would be his night to go out, and stay out. Then he could come home Tuesday morning.

He rented a one-room apartment on the eleventh floor of a building on Ocean Avenue. He put mirrors along one wall, to make it appear bigger. He put outdoor carpet on the corner balcony. He called it "The Yacht Club" and found two men to share the rent. He made a schedule so that each man could have the place two nights a week. He furnished sheets and towels and did the laundry once a week. Each man provided his own food and beverages. My father kept that apartment for more than twenty-five years. He seemed to really enjoy being the caretaker. When he finally surrendered the rent-controlled lease, my mother confessed to me that she had come to look forward to her one night a week alone.

Mother used the "free night" to go to classes or see her friends. She once went to San Francisco with Jo with the intention of trying a one-night-stand. But in the end she couldn't do it. She was a one-man-woman and never had any desire to sleep with anyone but Peter.

Unfortunately for Benjie, Jo was not as accommodating as my mother. She did not want to share him. When he opened up to her she said two words, "Get out."

Jo got herself an ornery Siamese cat and continued to paint, design clothes and entertain. The other woman divorced her husband and married Benjie. They moved to a house in Pacific Palisades where Benjie continued to write stories and screenplays. They lived happily together until Benjie died of prostate cancer January 13, 2000.

The night I had dinner with Jo in August 1968, it was just me, her and Mama Cat. I walked up the steep steps of the little stucco building next to the Golden Bull restaurant's parking lot. The staircase was wedged between a beach-ware shop and Jo's Gallery. The small landing had a door on the left to an apartment where musician Ry Cooder lived. Jo's door, on the right, was covered in red and white flowered fabric. I jangled the Indian brass bells and opened the door.

Grass matting covered the floor. Benjie's tiny desk was still on the left, less his typewriter. Jo's sewing table and sewing machine were under the big window that looked out over a half-block of one-story buildings, the highway, the ocean. A line of colored threads on big cone-shaped bobbins lined the window sill.

Jo came out of her little red kitchen and gave me a hug. She wore her usual brightly colored caftan and coin jewelry. Her short, blond, tousled hair contrasted with her suntanned face. Jo had several face lifts over the years which gave her an impish expression.

"Come, come!" she said, herding me into the living room, "dinner is almost ready!"

I sat at the low, round, marble table, on a batik pillow. A clear flat-bottomed glass bowl held spears of crisp romaine. I could see salad dressing in the bottom of the bowl.

"I got the recipe from Sunset Magazine." Jo said. "It's called Stand-Up Salad."

She went back into the kitchen and came out with two square wooden plates. She set them on the table, went back to the kitchen for her rum and Coke and brought me iced tea in a thick green glass.

"Yum," I said tasting Jo's homemade enchiladas.

"I use spaghetti sauce and add chili powder," Jo said.

For an hour we ate and talked. Jo wanted to know all about my life, living on my own, my friends, my work, my boyfriends.

When we got to my parents Jo said, "Your parents have what Benjie and I had, a symbiotic relationship. It means you're like one person. This is why Alice will never leave Peter. She has no identity away from him."

"But you kicked Benjie out," I said.

"I did," Jo replied. She looked out the front windows, over a row of bright red geraniums. "I could not share him. I cried for three weeks, every day. But I know that it was not healthy to be that close to another person. I thought I could tell Benjie what to do, what to think. But that's not healthy. I love him. I truly do and will always love him. I have to let him be himself and have the kind of love life he has with . . ." her voice trailed off and she got tears in her eyes. She wiped her eyes. "Don't let a man take over your life, Mary Lee."

I gazed down at my plate. I *wanted* to be in love and give my life over to someone else. I was the happiest in my life when I was I love with Lenny, before he broke my heart. I still felt in love with Marc, secretly hoping we could end up together someday. Wasn't that the way love worked, that two people wanted to become one? It was all so confusing.

"Come!" Jo said, getting up. She was very limber and fit for a sixty-three-year old. Every morning she drove up to Ocean Avenue and did yoga stretches on the grass.

I got up and followed her into her bedroom with its bright yellow walls, Indian canopy over the bed, and aquarium. Along one wall dark corkboard held photographs of all her friends, famous and not so famous, including many pictures of me and my family. Jo went through a beaded curtain into her closet and came out with several new garments. "Try these on," she said.

I pulled off my shirt and stepped out of my pants. I stepped into a floor length patchwork skirt with a red waistband. I slipped a gauzy cropped top over my head. "Perfect!" Jo said.

"Did you make these just for me?" I asked.

"The skirt, yes. The top is a prototype for a line I'm working on. I want to make the sleeves a little longer."

"Thank you!" I said, hugging her. "Where's your kitty?"

"On the balcony," Jo said. The glass bedroom door was ajar. I stepped outside. Mama Cat was sleeping on the turquoise banquette. On the other side of the concrete storm drain I could see the apartment Mother and I had lived in last year. My life had changed a lot since then.

My mind was teeming with questions. I wanted to ask Jo how I could fall in love, but not lose myself. And how could I trust whoever I loved to not fall in love with someone else? Why was I still in love with Marc even though we weren't really together? How many more times would my heart be broken before I found a man to love me? I sat on the banquette next to the sleepy Siamese.

"Hi Mama cat," I said. She opened one eye, then put her paw over her face.

Later in the week I had dinner with my parents at Casa Mia, our favorite Mexican restaurant down the block from Jo's apartment. I sat facing them in the green vinyl booth. I ordered a *chile relleno*. I loved they way they cooked them, not battered, just a fresh green chili with cheese on top, broiled to golden brown perfection.

"I was thinking," Mother said, "it would be fun to do a book together—of your poems and our pictures."

I perked up. I loved projects and working as a team. This was the first summer in four years that I wasn't in a play and I missed it. Since I started writing poems in high school, I'd let Mother read many of them.

"How many poems to you have now?" she asked.

"About twenty-five, I guess." I answered.

"What do you think, Peter?" she asked him.

"Sounds like fun. I'll use two-and-a-quarter film . . ."

"Why don't we do some tests and send them into Crown?" Mother said. "They've been wonderful publishing our other books. I'm sure they'll like it. It's very timely. I just read a review of a best-selling poet named Rod McKuen. In my opinion, your poems are better than his." She bit into her crispy taco.

"I can't do it for a couple of weeks, though," my dad said. My mother and I looked at each other. We knew what that meant. He would be "out of town" with his mistress.

As the summer wore on, I spent more time with Linda and Chrissie spent more time with her own group of friends. One day one of Chrissie's male friends came to the house. He offered me a "downer," some sort of tranquilizer. I had no desire to try it. I liked to get high on drugs that stimulated my mind and made me more creative. Lolling around didn't appeal to me.

"How can you call yourself a poet, if you won't even try it?" he asked.

"I call myself a poet because I write poems," I answered. I grabbed my car keys and headed off to Linda's apartment.

That Sunday Chrissie and I planned to see *2001 a Space Odyssey*, playing at the gaudy Egyptian Theater in Hollywood. We invited Joanne and Linda. We met at our house to drop mescaline, figuring it would start taking affect in about half-an-hour, the time it took to drive to Hollywood. The four of us gathered in our little kitchen and I passed out the big, white capsules. I felt like we were members of a secret society about to have a spiritual experience together.

I sat in the back with Linda. Joanne sat in front. Chrissie drove her big blue Ford Fairlane. She took Sunset Boulevard. By the time we got to West Hollywood my stomach felt queasy. She pulled over and Linda ran into a drug store and bought me some Pepto-Bismal tablets. I chewed the pink chalky triangles and almost gagged but they did help settle my stomach.

We made it to the theater parking lot and walked down the terrazzo sidewalk to the ticket booth. Stepping in to the lobby, we were all overcome by its grandeur.

"Feel this velvet!" Joanne said as she stroked one of the thick blood-red curtains. The smell of buttered popcorn surrounded us. My mouth watered. I felt frozen in my tracks.

"Come on!" Linda said, pulling me. "The movie is about to start." We followed her into the dimly lit theater. Every seat seemed to be taken. "This way," she said heading up steep stairs. The stairs were steeper than any stairs I had ever climbed. I didn't think my feet could lift that high. I sat down on a step.

"What are you doing?" whispered Chrissie, taking my hand and pulling me up. "Keep going!"

I let her pull me up to the very last row. We inched our way past people who seemed annoyed and found four seats together in the middle of the row. I collapsed into my seat. When I looked out toward the gigantic screen I felt that I might float right out of my seat. I clung to the arm rests. I turned to look at Joanne beside me. She turned to look at me. Her eyes were as big as saucers.

Just then the music began, "Boom!" The four of us shrieked.

"Shut up!" someone below us called. The space between us and the screen seemed to disappear. We were not watching a movie, we were *in* the movie, but now it wasn't a movie at all, it was real and chimpanzees were banging big leg bones and shrieking. Or were *we* the ones shrieking? Or were we laughing? Yes, it was very funny. The funniest thing we had ever seen—monkeys banging bones. Ridiculous!

"Shhhh . . ." came a voice in the darkness. I squinted against a flashlight shown in my face. "Be quiet or you'll have to leave!" said a disembodied voice.

The next thing I knew Joanne was taking my hand and pulling me out of my chair. Then those steep, steep stairs. No way could I walk down them. They were too steep. I might fall. I sat down and one by one inched my way down the steps on my butt, until we got to level ground. I stood and followed my friends out of the theater into the lobby.

We kept going until we were out on the blindingly bright sidewalk. Terrible! Too bright. I clung to the side of the building as we walked toward the parking lot. A tiny alcove offered some shade.

"You can't stay in there," Chrissie said. But I just wanted to sit down and close my eyes and look at the beautiful colors dancing behind my eyelids. So this is where all color comes from, I thought. They're in your *mind*.

Somehow we found Chrissie's car. She unlocked the doors and we climbed in. I curled up in the back seat, against the door. I looked up at the roof and noticed the fine weave of the blue gray headliner. Beautiful!

Chrissie managed to get the key in the ignition. The engine turned over. So loud! The car vibrated like a stampede of horses.

"I don't remember how to back up," Chrissie said.

"I can drive," Linda said, opening the passenger door. Chrissie slid over into the passenger seat. Linda got behind the wheel. She put the car in reverse and slowly backed out of the parking space. She inched forward to the street. She made a left turn and then another left and we were back on Sunset Boulevard, driving five miles an hour.

"I don't think we took mescaline," Joanne said. "I think this is acid!"

"Roll down your window!" Linda barked at Chrissie and pulled over to the curb. Chrissie turned the crank on the window. A young bearded hitch hiker leaned in the window.

"We thought we took mescaline but now we think it's acid!" Linda told him. "Can you drive us home?"

"Where do you live?" he asked.

"Topanga," Chrissie told him.

"Well, I was headed to Venice, but I guess it's sort of on my way," he said. He walked around the car. Linda scooted over and he got in.

"Oh thank you so much!" Joanne said.

I studied the back of the hitch hikers head. His glossy hair fell in curvy waves. I noticed that although one might call him a brunette, his hair contained so many different shades of brown, some golden, others dark, like an animal's coat. I wondered why some hair is straight and other is curly. Why does the hair on our arms and legs stop growing and hair on the head grow and grow?

The hum of the engine and the smell of the hitchhiker's leather and dusty cotton mixed with Linda's patchouli and lulled me as we floated down Sunset Boulevard in the big blue Ford-boat to our cabin by the sea.

The kind hitchhiker took us home, then hitch hiked his way south to Venice. I spent an unknown length of time lying under a flowering bush, marveling at the intricacies of leaves, petals and tiny bugs who were unaware of a nineteen-year-old, stoned poet observing them.

On Wednesday, August 28th, Linda and I headed up the coast in her powder blue Volkswagen Beetle. I had never been further north than Santa Barbara and let her plan our week-long adventure. We spent the first night at Big Sur, dining on tempeh and brown rice at Nepenthe restaurant and inn, perched on the rocky cliffs. Pounding surf kept me awake most of the night.

Thursday we headed up to Asilomar, a conference center on the Monterrey Bay Peninsula. Here Linda handed me a "blue barrel" that was indeed LSD. We found comfortable places to recline on the white sand dunes and waited for the drug to take effect.

On my mescaline trips I'd created intricate pencil drawings, listened to beautiful music and mused about nature. I hoped that taking LSD in that beautiful place would turn me into some sort of wood nymph. But as the morning fog lifted, a great hollowness filled me. The sand dunes looked fake. Had Hollywood trucked in this sand? The boulders looked as fake as the papier mache-covered chicken wire boulder my dad lugged down to the beach. The pine trees looked plastic. The sky looked metallic. The sun looked like a big klieg light shining through a diffuser.

Inside I felt bruised and hollow. Why couldn't I feel like Linda, who was romping over the dunes, her strawberry blonde hair fanning out like a halo? I could hear her sing as her bright, long skirt billowed around her.

By nightfall we had come down from the LSD. We sat in our little room on our narrow beds. I just wanted to sleep. Linda lit a joint. I took a hit and perked up enough to recline against the knotty-pine wall while Linda drew me. She asked me to take off my shirt. I did. She let me talk about the sadness that welled up in me, as her pencil moved across the paper, capturing my sad expression.

The next day Linda and I browsed the quaint shops of Carmel-by-the-Sea and went to see *Gone with the Wind*. We met Linda's aunt, a professorial woman who had traveled extensively. She regaled us with stories about her many worldly adventures.

One evening we walked around the campus of U.C. Berkeley. I loved the huge old trees, their wonderful smell, and the ivy-covered brick buildings that looked like New England. The night air had a crispness I hadn't experienced in Southern California. I felt as if I were falling in love with this place—the University, the hills, the view of the San Francisco Bay, hippies, artists, intellectuals, Telegraph

Avenue crammed with bookstores and restaurants, pan-handlers, street musicians.

When Linda and I returned from our trip, Chrissie told me she planned to move out, mid-month. I asked Linda if she'd like to be my roommate. She said yes. On September 29th she and I went to a concert at the Rose Bowl with some friends of hers. I remember sitting in the stands and Linda saying, "Give me your skirt."

"What?" I asked.

"Come on, I want to borrow your skirt!" she said, taking my hand. I followed her to the restrooms. I took off my long flowered skirt and put on her black pants that were a little loose around the waist.

"What are you going to do?" I asked her.

"You'll see!" she said.

We left the bathroom. I headed back to our seats but Linda hung back. The concert started. Jefferson Airplane opened the show on a stage set up in the middle of the field. Only our side of the stadium was occupied.

Suddenly, down on the field behind the stage I saw Linda, running and leaping to the music, my flowered skirt billowing around her as she did arabesques and *tourgetes*. Her friends and I laughed. She sure had guts. Soon a black-clad security guard was chasing after her. They both disappeared behind the stage. A few minutes later Linda ascended the steep stadium steps, a grin the size of the Cheshire cat on her face. She bowed to the people around us, who gave her a standing ovation.

Over a period of two weeks Chrissie emptied her bedroom and Linda brought in her furniture. One evening, around dusk, Linda and I were sitting in the living room smoking a bong and listening to Buffy Saint Marie. Two quick taps on the door and Chrissie entered.

"Hi," she said. "I've come to get the rest of my stuff."

"Want a hit?" Linda asked.

"No, I can't. I'm driving" Chrissie said. She did a quick perusal of the house. I could hear kitchen drawers opening and closing.

Then she came into the living room, walked over to the window, reached up and grabbed the curtain rod. She lifted it up and carried it out the door. Linda and I sat looking out the window at the big orange rotating Gulf sign.

"I'll have to make us some curtains," Linda said, letting out a long stream of smoke.

Chapter 19

TOM

I had to find a boyfriend. My life would not be complete until I had someone to love and share my life with. Rex was an okay boyfriend for the summer but he was going back to school in the Valley and besides I had never been "in love" with him.

Linda had become a good friend but I wanted a *man* to share my psychedelic adventures. I wanted someone artistic, and smart. I wanted a boyfriend who could teach me things I didn't know. I wanted sex and I wanted to be monogamous.

The week before school started, the thought popped into my mind, *I'm going to meet him at SMCC.* I felt absolutely certain, which surprised me, because I thought the people who went to city college—myself included—were generally losers, a rag-tag bunch of misfits who hadn't gotten good enough grades to get into a "real" college.

The day school started I dressed in my wrap-around buckskin skirt, a dark orange tank top, my favorite brown, thin-strapped sandals with thick, one-inch heels. I tied an orange bandana around my neck.

As I was walking across the campus I saw "him" sitting under a sycamore tree, reading. He wore a long sleeved white shirt, black vest, white pants and brown fringed moccasins. Shiny brown hair fell to his shoulders. *There he is,* I thought.

I watched him for a few minutes, confident that I would find him again. On Friday I walked into my Poly-Sci class and there he was, with an empty seat beside him. I took the seat.

"Hi," I said cheerfully.

"Hello," he answered softly. One of his front teeth was chipped. His skin was pale, as if he spent all his time indoors. He had long artistic fingers, and long fingernails on his right hand.

"Do you play the guitar?" I asked.

"Yes," he answered and looked at his hands, then at me, and smiled. "I write my own songs." Bingo.

Class started so we stopped talking. When the class ended we stood up. He was tall, over six-feet and very thin. I looked up into his grey eyes and casually asked, "Do you happen to know where I can buy some mescaline?"

He paused a moment before he answered. "How much do you want?"

"Not a lot. A few hits." I said.

"I'll see what I can do." He replied.

"I'm Mary Lee," I said. "I'm a poet."

"I'm Tom," he told me. We stood a moment just looking at each other. Then he turned and headed for the door.

"See you next week," I called.

"Yeah," he said, turning. "Next week." I watched him join the throng of students in the hallway, hoping he didn't notice the big silly grin on my face.

True to his word, Tom followed through on my request. When I took the seat beside him the next week he said, "I was able to do that errand you requested."

"Oh, good!" I said cheerfully.

"It's at my apartment." He said. He seemed to be studying my face. "If you give me a ride home, you can pick it up."

"You didn't drive here?" I asked.

"I don't drive," he said.

"Ever?" I had never known anyone in Los Angeles who didn't drive.

"I don't have a car," he said. "I walk or take the bus or friends give me rides."

After class we walked to my car. He had to push the seat back to accommodate his long legs. I buckled the seatbelt around my waist and put the key in the ignition. I pulled out the choke.

"So you don't smoke?" Tom asked, looking at the No Smoking sticker I had put above the radio.

"Not tobacco," I answered, stepping on the clutch.

He lived just a few blocks from Linda's old apartment in Ocean Park. Several small cottages surrounded a central, grassy courtyard. Inside Tom had a single mattress on the floor, covered with a grey blanket, and a stereo on cinder blocks. Small speakers were mounted on the wall. Between them was a portrait of Jesus Christ. The rest of the furnishings consisted of several large pillows on the floor, a guitar on a stand, and a black amplifier with a gold-painted bust of Beethoven on top.

"Have a seat," Tom gestured toward the pillows. I sat cross-legged, covering my knees with my skirt.

Tom went into the kitchenette and opened the freezer. He came back, sat his gangly frame next to me and opened a cookie tin. He took out a plastic bag filled with white capsules. "How many do you want?" he asked.

"Um, I guess, two?" I replied. I'd used the request for mescaline just to get to know Tom better. I actually still had some of Eric's mescaline at home.

Tom used his long fingernails to pluck two capsules and set them in my outstretched palm. "On the house," he said. "Let me know how you like it."

"Thank you," I said. I tucked the capsules into my wallet.

"Would you like to smoke some pot and listen to music?" Tom asked.

"Your music?"

"No, I want to play some Beethoven for you," he said.

"All right," I said. I watched Tom take out some marijuana buds and break them apart on a shoebox lid. He tilted and shook the box top gently so that the seeds skittered down to the bottom. Then he filled a cigarette paper and artfully, with one hand, rolled a joint. When he licked the paper and sealed the joint, I wondered what it would be like to kiss him.

After the first hit I knew the pot was strong, so I shook my head when he offered me a second one. I leaned back against the pillows and felt my heart pounding in my ears. Tom took two hits then snuffed out the joint. He set a record on his turntable and lowered the needle.

The room was filled with the strains of dozens of violins. Then other orchestral instruments joined in. I closed my eyes. I felt as if I were floating in music. Images of rolling meadows, flowers and flocks of birds filled my mind as Beethoven's Sixth Symphony, known as the *Pastoral* filled the tiny room.

I lost track of time. I forgot my surroundings. During the passage that sounds like a thunderstorm the room seemed to get markedly cooler. I'd always loved music but I had never experienced it quite like this. I wanted more.

When I opened my eyes, Tom was standing over the turntable, lifting the needle.

He turned and looked at me with raised eyebrows.

"Wow," I said. "That was beautiful."

"I've gone through all of Beethoven and now I'm working backwards through Mozart to Bach."

"Are you taking a music class?"

"No, I'm doing it on my own. Really good musicians study the classics. That's why the Beatles and the Beach Boys are so good. They understand harmonics. They know how to listen."

Outside the day had grown dark. "I better get going," I said. "I don't like driving at night."

"Where do you live?" Tom asked.

"Topanga."

"Where's that?"

"Topanga?" I said. "up the coast, just past the Palisades, the beginning of Malibu. You've never been to Malibu? Where are you from?"

"Milwaukee," he said. "I've only been here a few months. Mostly I spend my time in Hollywood. I'm not really a beach person. I can't swim."

"Milwaukee." I said, feeling the word in my mouth. He might just as well have said the moon. I had never known anyone from the mid-west. "Bet it gets cold there."

"That it does," Tom said and smiled.

Linda and I took Tom's mescaline and spent an evening drawing and listening to our favorite records—Donovan, Bob Dylan, Janis Joplin, and of course the Beatles.

At school the next week I reported to Tom that Linda and I had liked the mescaline. When class ended the two of us stayed behind.

"I wrote you a poem," I said. I took the folded page out of my binder and handed it to him.

Tom opened it up. "It's a sonnet," he said. I was surprised and happy that he knew the form. I had intentionally written a poem with a lot of questions in it, so he would have to answer them.

> My skins not black and yet I feel if I
> Were to descend the icy night that not
> A single soul should see me passing by
> His eyes. Would you? Or would you too be caught
> Inside the earth or stars and never feel

What's in between? It's of no consequence.
For if I ever pass, you'll know I'm real
And sight or sound will not be influenced
To make seem true what isn't there. I'll just
Appear in darkness or in light and you
Can speak in hollow tones until I trust
Your reason, but is reason always true?
Can words express my needs and wants in terms
Of their intensity? Will deeds confirm?

"You wanna come over this weekend?" Tom said in response to the poem. "Take some M. and listen to music? You can spend the night, since you don't like driving in the dark."

Making love with Tom felt like I was hugging an ironing board. He seemed to weigh practically nothing. Shy in bed, he was not sensual, like Marc, nor athletic like Rex. He finished before the first movement of Vivaldi's *Four Seasons* was over. But I didn't mind. What had great sex gotten me, except heartache? Tom and I were so completely different, in our history and our tastes that I knew I would learn many things from him.

When we got hungry Tom served chipped beef on toast, something I had never eaten. As he heated it up I glanced through the *Pictorial History of the World*, a green, well-worn, leather bound volume Tom had gotten for Christmas when he was twelve. I liked that he was interested in music and history and religion, particularly mysticism. Another of his books, *Self-Unfoldment by Disciplines of Realization* by Manly Palmer Hall, published by the Philosophical Research Society of Los Angeles, reminded me of my grandmother, Andy's, metaphysical books.

As we sat on the floor and ate, Tom talked a little bit about being a neglected child. He had an older, married sister living in Milwaukee, but both his parents were dead. Lying side by side in his narrow bed, I felt the desire to take care of Tom. I'd feed him fresh, healthy food and bring fun and happiness into his life. In exchange he would teach me so much I didn't know, about music and the world.

For the first photo shoot for my book of poems—which didn't have a title yet—we used my parents' studio. Mother put me in an old lace slip and had me sit on a black background, with my hands in my lap, looking sad. This became the first picture in the book. A few more shots from that day were also used.

Then we went down to State Beach. Mother staged the shots and my dad took pictures of me walking across the Polio Pond with sunlight sparkling on the water, and coming out of the underpass, dark shadows and light creating crisp geometric patterns.

"We need a young man in the pictures," Mother said. "What about this new boy you're seeing?"

"I hardly know him!" I said. "Besides, the poems are mostly about Marc, about him breaking my heart. I thought this was going to be just me and my poems."

"I agree with Mother," my father said. "This book is a love story. There needs to be a love interest. Nobody's going to know the poems were written to someone else."

I planned to talk to Tom after school. But as I walked toward the classroom I found him waiting for me in the hall.

"I need to talk to you," he said, taking my elbow. We walked out of the building to a secluded spot. "I can't go home. I sent a friend of mine some weed and he got busted with it. I'm afraid my house is being watched."

My heart began to race. I looked over my shoulder to see if anyone could hear us.

"Can I come home with you tonight?" Tom asked.

My mouth was so dry I could hardly answer. "Sure," I finally said. "But let's go to class now . . ."

"I'll meet you afterwards, here," he said, and walked away.

I had a hard time concentrating in class. A friend of mine had dated a guy who tried to ship kilos of marijuana inside a hollow surfboard and got busted. What if Tom got busted? What if I got busted for aiding and abetting him?

After class I found Tom waiting for me in the hall. We walked to my car. "I want to stop and pick up a few things," he said.

"Are you sure it's safe?" I asked.

"I think it's okay, for now." He said he had a friend in Hollywood he could stay with if I was too scared. The friend was also from Milwaukee and was the one who told him about their mutual friend getting busted. "As long as my friend doesn't rat me out, I'll be okay. I don't think he will, but I'd rather not sit home and wait for a cop to bang on my door."

On the drive to Topanga I decided to tell Tom about the book I was working on with my parents. Would he be willing to be in some pictures?

"I'm not a model," Tom said.

"I'm not asking you to model. Just come with me. It'll be fun. My parents are really easy to be around. You'll like them."

I was thrilled to find that Linda and Tom liked each other. She liked him because he played chess and stayed up late. After I'd gone to bed I could hear them talking softly in the living room. It reminded me of when I was little and I could hear my parents talking and laughing with Jo and Benjie, after I'd gone to bed.

I don't remember who brought up Tom moving in, me, him or Linda. We just seem to fall into an easy routine and liked being together. I took him back to his cottage and we loaded up my Volkswagen with his clothes, guitar, books and excellent dope.

One night Tom and I took mescaline and listened to Beethoven's Sixth Symphony, sitting on my Indian-bedspread-canopied bed. With my eyes closed I felt like we were two eighteenth century aristocrats riding through our estate, past fields and streams, dressed like Gainsborough's Mr. and Mrs. Andrews.

On October 20th, I took Tom to meet my parents.

"This is nothing like Milwaukee," he said as we drove over the wooden bridge. The front door was unlocked. Mother was talking on the kitchen phone. She smiled and waved us in. Tom gazed around at the indoor planters, view of the canyon, the terrazzo floor. I took him into the studio. He looked up at the big bounce-flash umbrella hanging from the ceiling and said, "Wow."

We found my father in the darkroom, loading his Hasselblad. "This is Tom," I said. My dad extended his hand.

"Pleased to meet you," Tom said. How strange to see the two most important men in my life together. The only things they had in common (besides me) were their height and the fact that they were both handsome; my dad tan, athletic, and Tom pale, ascetic. My father represented my past, Tom represented my future.

Tom seemed embarrassed by the nude pictures on the walls of the front office. I remembered when Susie Beck saw the pictures and told me I probably wouldn't go to hell but my father would. I was so used to seeing these pictures they didn't phase me. I had to remember that not everyone grew up like I did.

That afternoon my mother took us out into the backyard and posed Tom and me on the hill behind the house. My dad took close ups and long shots, of me and Tom and me alone.

The next week Mother submitted thirty of my poems and the first sets of pictures to Crown. On December 6th she got a phone call. Our book had been accepted. Millan Brand, author and poet would be my editor. At the time I didn't know who he was. I knew very little of modern American poets and poetry. However, my parents were pleased, because besides being an anti-war activist, Millan Brand had written the screenplay for *The Snake Pit*, the drama in which my grandmother Andy had a bit part. Millen wanted more poems and more pictures. The plan was to have fifty poems. So I started writing every day whether I was in the mood, or not.

For a while my life in Topanga with Linda and Tom was perfect. Linda painted, Tom wrote songs, I wrote poems. We took psychedelics. The two of them played chess.

On New Year's Eve the three of us visited my lonely father. Mother had gone out with Jo. His mistress had to work.

The four of us sat in the living room and toasted the new year by lighting a joint. Linda passed it to my father, who took a drag and started coughing. We all laughed. He tried again and this time inhaled more.

I looked around at the house that was no longer my home. My nine-year-old black cat had disappeared a few months after I moved away. Mother said he kept jumping up on her desk when she was trying to work, so she put him outside. That was the last she saw of him. I entertained fantasies that he wandered off to another home where he could have the kind of attention I always gave him.

The black-and-white TV in the corner was on, with the sound off. I could see happy revelers in Times Square ringing in 1969. But I had no desire to be there. I was glad to be right here, in the cricket-filled canyon with my new friend, my new love and my new life, as a published poet, before me.

After a while we got up to leave. Tom and I walked out to Linda's car. Just as I was turning to wave goodbye to my dad, I saw Linda put her arms around him and give him a big kiss on the mouth. *Gross*, I thought, shaking my head.

Then Linda came down the stairs and I saw my father standing alone. He looked like a sad nine-year-old boy whose father just dropped him off at military school, and I felt sorry for him.

Chapter 20

TENDER BOUGH

Millen Brand decided to change a word in one of my sonnets. The original line was "One gentle bough stripped naked, almost lifeless in the chill of dusk, as dust upon a windowsill." He wanted it to read "one *tender* bough stripped naked . . ." and use *Tender Bough* as the book title.

I hated it. *It sounds like something to eat,* I thought.

My parents usually received a ten-percent royalty on their photography books. Now Crown sent two contracts, one to them and one to me, with each of us getting a five-percent royalty. The paperback edition of *Tender Bough* listed for $1.95. That meant we each got less than ten cents per copy.

Up until now my mother had not gotten credit on the twenty-some books she had written with my dad. She was happy to be "the woman behind the man." She took his first drafts and rewrote them, in his voice. No one ever suspected it was she who actually wrote the published works.

Now, in 1969, things had changed. Their marriage had changed. Mother was more independent. She liked the idea when I suggested she get co-credit. After all, the book was her idea and she was designing most of the shots.

So the book would be *Tender Bough, Fifty Poems by Mary Lee Gowland, with Photographs by Alice and Peter Gowland.* Wait a minute. Did I want people to know that my parents had taken the pictures of me and my boyfriend? No. I thought it would be better if readers thought I was a young poet who had somehow gotten a world famous photography team to take pictures for me. So I decided to drop my last name and be known by one name, like Cher or Charo. But everyone ended up thinking Mary was my first name and Lee, my last. Oh, well.

Now we had a deadline. Three more photo sessions ensued: at Rustic Canyon Park; in a vacant lot full of wild mustard up on Ocean Avenue; and in my parents' backyard, where my father created an outdoor shower. Mother poured a bucket of water over Tom and me, as we knelt on the pavement by the pool.

In February, 1969, I started having terrible pain in my mouth. My bottom wisdom teeth were impacted. I decided to have all four out at once—just get it over with! If I had the teeth pulled on Wednesday, I should be okay by the Monday, finals week.

By now Linda was hanging out with a new group of friends. After all, I was busy with Tom and my book. Her friends had a dog and litter of lab-mix puppies, about three months old. Linda's dog had run away while she was still living in Ocean Park. She planned to keep one of the puppies.

One day Linda and her friends ate peyote buttons. I walked into her room to find people sprawling on the bed and floor, with huge, dilated eyes.

"We took peyote and are throwing up out the window," Linda said breathlessly. This sort of tripping didn't appeal to me. I closed her bedroom door and Tom and I went to a movie.

On the day of my oral surgery, I left my car at my parents' house and Mother drove me to the appointment. The doctor looked like a body builder. He gave me a sedative. I watched the curtains start to undulate. The last thing I remember is the doctor hovering over me with those huge arms, then a horrible tugging and the rusty taste of blood.

I could barely walk to the car. I was in such a groggy stupor. I woke up in my old bedroom, momentarily disoriented. For a brief instant I thought I was sixteen again, in love with Lenny. Then the pain hit. I've never experienced such pain, as if my head had been bashed in. I swallowed some codeine pills and tried to sleep.

I spent the next two days mostly sleeping. I wasn't hungry but Mother insisted I try to drink liquids. Little pockets where my teeth had been were stuffed with bloody gauze. I had holes in my jaws for many months afterwards.

Linda came to visit and dropped off Tom. He slept on the floor beside me, on the foam mattress my dad used to sunbathe outside. That night a huge winter storm arrived causing mudslides all along Pacific Coast Highway. The road was closed from Santa Monica to Malibu.

I didn't know at the time that Linda and her friends had gone to a party at her dad's house and left the puppies locked in the house at Topanga. She thought they'd be home that night, but they were stranded in Santa Monica.

Tom and I got back to the house before they did. The puppies had gotten into the garbage and scattered it all over the house. They had pooped and peed on the floor and climbed into my bed, which was now a muddy mess of torn sheets. They had gotten out of the house, by my bedroom door, but luckily had not run away. Some of my shoes were chewed.

Tom and I walked through the dog-destroyed house in a stupor. His amplifier lay on its side, the gold Beethoven bust was on the floor, chipped. I salvaged a roll of my drawings from the floor of my closet where some of the puppies had been sleeping. I bagged the garbage, fed and watered the dogs. Tom and I grabbed some clothes and headed back to my parents' house.

We immediately started looking for somewhere else to live. Linda and her gang could have the Topanga house. I didn't want to go back there. Tom and I rented a one-bedroom apartment on a cul-du-sac in Ocean Park, a white stucco duplex. My mom and dad didn't say whether they approved of me living with Tom, but Mother did say, "Now that you're living with your boyfriend we won't be paying your rent." I wasn't worried. The apartment was cheaper than the Topanga house. And Tom, well he'd just have to pay his share.

We put our mattress on the linoleum floor in the bedroom. After a week the mattress emitted a horrible stench that seemed to come up from under the house. We named it the Salami Monster and moved the mattress into the living room. The smelly bedroom remained empty, just a path to the bathroom.

The apartment and the neighborhood were a huge come-down from Topanga. I missed the pretty trees and the ocean across the street. But it was winter, so we spent most of our time inside anyway. Plus, it was closer to town, for work. So, even though Ruskin Street was one of the most depressing places I ever lived, it served us well.

Tom didn't care about clothes, or going out to clubs. He spent his extra money on records, specifically Deutche Grammaphone albums. He methodically took us through various eras and countries. We liked the more restrained, older music better, the structure and order. I grew to love counterpoint in Bach, as if two people were having an ongoing argument or lively conversation. I learned to appreciate the "frilliness" of Mozart. When I put myself in that mindset—everything at that time was dripping with folderol, clothing, furniture, carriages, those ridiculous powdered wigs—then I was able to appreciate Mozart's genius and take in all those notes in their intricate patterns.

Tom and I also listened to Debussey and Ravel and read Lord Byron and the Romantic poets. I didn't like *The Planets*, or *Pictures at an Exhibition*, but Tom felt they should be part of our curriculum. Vivaldi's *Four Seasons* and Handel's *Water Music* were diversions that didn't particularly take my breath away like Mozart's later symphonies and operas. I think we must have memorized *The Magic Flute*. We even saved our money and went to see a performance at the Dorothy Chandler Pavilion, downtown.

Tom and I didn't go to church but we had our Sunday ritual: we'd have a little breakfast then "drop" LSD or psilocybin or mescaline. I'd wear my antique, long-sleeved, white nightgown. Tom would put a stack of records on the turntable, starting with oldest first.

We'd lie on my little fake Persian rug, pillows under our heads and only get up to drink or pee, between albums. Music filled our minds for six straight hours. By late afternoon, coming down, we'd smoke a few hits of marijuana to come back up again, and listen to The Beatles while we heated soup on the little gas stove.

We had no TV so we read a lot. We both read a biography of Mozart and I kept track of which of his compositions we had heard. We read the Bible and tried to decipher the Book of Revelation. He felt very strongly that we were coming to the End of Times and should get out of L.A. before the shit hit the fan. Prophets were predicting a big earthquake would strike California and half of it would sink into the sea, just like the lost civilization of Atlantis.

I tried not to think about falling into the ocean. I focused on finding work. The Gruners had hired someone to work fulltime, when I had gone back to school the previous fall. I got a job at a dress shop on the Third Street Mall, but only lasted a few weeks. I didn't like standing around waiting for customers to show up. My Screen Extras Guild dues were paid up, so I took a couple days work on a movie called *The Phynx*.

Here's the premise: Johnny Weismuller (famous for his role as Tarzan, and our neighbor on Latimer road) has been kidnapped and taken to Albania along with a host of other actors and celebrities including Maureen O'Sullivan, James Brown, Colonel Sanders, Rudy Vallee, Xavier Cougat, Dick Clark, Butterfly McQueen and writer Rhona Barrett. A rock band, called the Phynx, consisting of a black model, American Indian, athlete and campus militant, is formed to rescue them from the Communists. After the premier, studio heads at Warner Brothers decided it was so awful they didn't release it. I think nowadays such "bombs" go direct to DVD.

My parents worked on a public service movie, about keeping the beaches clean, my dad as cameraman, Mother as producer. I got to be one of the extras running down the beach after Jonathan Winters. Several times we had to stop filming because Winters was so funny adlibbing he cracked us all up.

As an Extra I made $35.00 a day, which was more than three times the minimum wage, $1.30 an hour. Tom contributed by dealing drugs. I remember the first time he bought a kilo(2.2 pounds) of marijuana, for $100.00. He used the bathtub to break it up and measure out thirty-five one-ounce bags (lids). One kilo netted $350.00, or $250.00 profit. Tom sold mostly to other musicians, who'd stop by to jam with him and buy some dope. I heard a lot of good music in that little stinky apartment. Of course we kept some pot for ourselves, but by selling just one kilo a month, Tom covered his share of the rent utilities and food.

On March 8th my sister Ann and six-year-old niece Tracy moved to San Francisco. I was sad to see them go, but PSA (Pacific Southwest Airlines) had a stand-by midnight flight from LAX to San Francisco for $15.00. So if I didn't want to do the six-hour drive, I could always fly up for a quick visit.

On March 21st Tom got a letter from his sister in Milwaukee. I handed him the envelope. He opened it and found another envelope inside from the Selective Service Administration telling him to report for his induction physical.

"I have to let them know I'm out of town and reschedule," he said.

"Then what?" I wanted to know.

"Then I'm going to get out on a medical deferment."

"'Meaning what?'"

"I'll get my weight under one-twenty and be disqualified."

Tom was already skinny. And we didn't eat much. He ate mostly the foods he grew up on: chipped beef on toast, macaroni, canned soup. Food didn't interest him. It was something he had to do to keep going.

The next day he opened his palm and showed me two pills.

"What are those?" I asked.

"Diet pills. So I won't get hungry.

"Can I try one? Just to see what it's like?" He handed me one. I spent the day painting our forest-green kitchen white. By 11:00 p.m. I was still wide awake.

The next day I felt like I'd been hit by a truck. I never took another diet pill. Tom also felt terrible. He said he would do a grape fast instead.

"Grape fast?" I asked.

"Yeah," he said. "They'll give me sugar for energy."

By the time another Selective Service letter arrived, two weeks later, Tom had already lost ten pounds. His new physical date was set for April 25th, three weeks away.

One unseasonably warm day we went to the beach. I could hardly look at his bony white body. He looked like he'd been in a concentration camp.

One day Tom's friend Mitchell showed up. He's the one who got busted with the pot Tom had mailed. Mitchell was only given a "slap on the wrist," and had not ratted on Tom. Mitchell was on his way to Dunsmuir, a little town four hours north of San Francisco in the Shasta Mountains. He said there were hippies living in secret tunnels in the mountain, preparing for the Apocalypse. Tom told him that after he flunked his physical, we'd join him.

I took Tom to the airport on Tuesday, April 1st. He would stay with his sister in Milwaukee and starve himself until his physical on April 25th. A few days later, when I talked to Mother, she told me she'd talked to Millen Brand, my editor at Crown. He would love to meet me. Mother wanted to buy me a ticket to New York to meet him, and on the way I could stop in Milwaukee and see Tom. In New York I could visit Kathie, who would be on spring break from college. Hooray!

I left for Milwaukee on April 16th, Mother's forty-ninth birthday. Tom's sister greeted me warmly and made up a room for me upstairs. Tom would sleep downstairs. I didn't tell her Tom wasn't really able to have sex, since he'd been starving himself. Even before that, our relationship was much more mental than physical. She didn't want us to set a bad example for her children. I felt sad, not being able to cuddle with my emaciated song writer. I laid awake most of the night, praying Uncle Sam would reject him.

I spent three days in Milwaukee. Tom's sister leant me her car so Tom and I could go to the botanical gardens, the art museum, and see *The Lion in Winter.* Having grown up in Southern California I almost cried when Tom's four-year-old niece, who had been playing outside, came into the kitchen and said, "Mommy, I need my mittens." It was forty degrees outside. The coldest winter I had ever experience in L.A. was about fifty degrees. I thought this was child abuse, to make your little girl go outside, when it was so cold!

I left Tom on March 20, flew to New York and took a cab to Kathie's parents' apartment. I was greeted with open arms and spent a happy evening watching the Tony Awards in her father's den. I was so happy to be reunited with my old friend and her family.

The next day Kathie, her sister Marie, and I went to see *Yellow Submarine* and eat delicious Jewish food at Carnegie Deli. The day after that I went to Crown Publishers. I met my editor, and got the grand tour. Millan Brand, a grey-haired intellectual in a tweed jacket, said of the fifty-one poems I'd sent him, he was going to use fifty.

I took the subway alone to meet my mother's cousin, a career woman in her late twenties, in Greenwich Village. I was blown away by the sights and sounds of the big city. In California everyone drove to their destinations. Here I jostled with thousands of others, as we scurried through the subway station. My cousin's apartment was one tiny room. I knew I could never live in a place with so much activity. I missed sleepy Santa Monica.

The day after I came home from New York, I went to LAX to pick up Tom. I met him at the gate, and carried his guitar. He was even more pale than before and unbelievably skinny. His eyes looked huge, sunk in his face. I wondered if I should have ordered a wheelchair.

"We're going to be vegetarians from now on," he told me in the car. "The day of my physical I came home and my sister put a big raw steak under my nose and asked me how I'd like her to cook it. But it just made me want to puke. It was so disgusting and bloody."

I didn't know much about vegetarianism. I started shopping at a health food store and tried to find meat substitutes. Mostly we ate brown rice, spinach and yams.

On May first I worked as an extra in the movie *Airport.* I got to wear a beautiful camel's hair coat. My assignment: stand with my back to the camera and stare out a window while Helen Hayes and her entourage pass through the terminal.

It took a whole day to shoot that one scene. During breaks everyone stood around, chatting. Many extras knew each other. They all talked about which stars they'd seen. I didn't want to end up like the fifty-five-year-old woman whose claim to fame was being in a scene with Clark Gable when she was thirty-five. And I didn't like being indoors under artificial lights, in the huge sound stages. Everything was too big. I missed working in an office with only a few people in the room at a time. No, being an extra was not for me. However, we were served lunch and I stuffed myself on foods that were now taboo at home.

Tom started having a lot of trouble, or I should say *more* trouble, with his teeth. He was in pain and could only eat soft foods. I wonder if that's the real reason he decided we should give up meat? I took him to a dentist who gave us an estimate on what it would cost to fix his teeth: more than either of us had.

A couple came into our lives, Sharon and Hank. They lived in an upstairs apartment in an old Spanish building in Westwood. I remember the long flight of stairs up to their door. We walked into the large, empty living room—just wall-to-wall striped rug and many comfortable pillows. Hank showed us a tray of colored glass bottles with the corks on the bottom. Each was filled with a different type of marijuana or hashish. It was like going to the cosmetic counter at Bullock's sniffing delicious perfumes. One smelled sweet, one smoky, another flowery. I chose what Hank said was Himalayan hash. He used his fingernail to take a pea-sized piece and place it in a big ornate bong. From the kitchen, petite, dark-haired Sharon brought a tray of fresh strawberries, sour cream and brown sugar, each in individual bowls. We dipped a strawberry in sour cream, then the brown sugar: heaven! From Hank Tom bought a bag of LSD to sell.

I teetered down the stairs, still very stoned. There, in the cul-du-sac were three cop cars with their red lights flashing. I almost fainted. I thought sure they had come to bust Hank.

"Be cool," Tom whispered behind me.

I managed to unlock my car door and get in. I leaned across the passenger seat to unlock Tom's door. My hands shook. My mouth was so dry I could hardly swallow. (These were the days before everyone carried around a bottle of water!) I took a deep breath and slowly drove down the street and back to Santa Monica. I never did find out why the cops had been there.

I worked on one more movie, *The Mod Squad,* before I finally found a full-time job at Executive Travel Agency in Beverly Hills. Six or seven travel agents all worked in one big room. I had no experience in the travel business but I was told soon I would receive training. In the meantime all I had to do was answer the phones.

At lunch I'd walk across to a little park and read the *Book of Mormon.* After three weeks the owner told me he had to let me go. It wasn't my fault. They were just too busy to train me. He needed an experienced travel agent, not a receptionist.

My parents, Tom and I did another photo shoot for *Tender Bough.* Tom and I lay on the studio floor and my dad stood over us to take the pictures. By now Tom was more comfortable, more relaxed and enjoyed my dad's banter.

Jo Lathwood's Siamese had a litter of kittens. I decided I wanted one. I picked out a feisty little male and named him Padma Sambhava, after the Buddhist saint. Tom called him Boscoe. The cat was a terror from the start. He liked to run up Tom's jeans, sharp claws puncturing the denim and leaving scratches on Tom's skinny legs. Tom had to kick him off.

I hadn't had my cat for over a year. And I hadn't had a kitten in almost ten years. Maybe I'd just forgotten how wild kittens could be. Eventually he'd simmer down. I hoped.

In July our life changed again in two ways. First, I got a full time job, at the Sheffield Watch Company showroom downtown, at the California Clothing Mart, where I used to work for the Gruners. My new boss was a traveling salesman, gone most of the time. Buyers seldom showed up. I answered the phone and tagged the broken watches the postman delivered in three or four huge canvas sacks. I wrote up repair orders and carried them over to a repair shop, a few blocks away. It took about two hours. The rest of the time I studied astrology from a Rosecrucian mail-order course. I had fun doing horoscopes of everyone I knew and learning more about myself.

Second, Tom, Bosco Kitty and I moved from the stinky apartment up to Beverly Glen. Beverly Glen Canyon runs from Sunset Boulevard, just east of UCLA, to Sherman Oaks in the San Fernando Valley. It's the southern boundary of Beverly Hills. Tom's friend Rudy rented a large, cantilevered studio on a steep hillside. It had a long deck above the gorge, a tiny kitchen and a small bathroom with a cement shower stall.

Up the hill was a smaller wooden artist studio, a shack really, with a sink but no running water. Tom and I rented this as our bedroom and had access to Rudy's kitchen and bathroom. During the day, while Rudy and I were at work—he managed a bookstore in Westwood—Tom worked on his music in the "big house." At night the three of us usually ate together, and talked. Then Tom and Rudy read or played chess and I drew or wrote poems for my second book. We also listened to a lot of music on the stereo: classical, folk, rock and roll.

I usually went to bed before Tom. I'd put on my antique white, long-sleeved nightgown and cowboy boots and carry my flashlight as I hiked up the steep dirt hillside and across a wooden plank.

Living in the wild canyon did not make Kitty more tame. One night, I'd just gotten into bed (a mattress on the floor) when I heard faint scratching. Not wanting to turn on the flashlight, I sat up and said, "Kitty, is that you?"

He jumped right onto my face. I screamed and pushed him off of me. Huddling under the covers I scolded, "I'm not a mouse!" I laid very still so he wouldn't attack my feet.

The first weekend in August, Tom and I dropped acid. I remember standing on the high studio deck: blinding white sunlight, heat bearing down, the buzz of insects and bright orange and yellow spears of gladiolas all around the deck, like some giant alien flowers. Suddenly, the still summer air was shattered by the horrible din of a police helicopter swooping through the canyon. What now? A dread flooded through me. Maybe Tom's friend Mitchell was right—we should get out before things got worse.

The next morning on the front page of the *Los Angeles Times:* Sharon Tate, the beautiful actress/wife of movie director Roman Polanski and some of her friends had been murdered the day before, in the next canyon over. The helicopters I'd heard and seen were part of the search for the group of people purported to have committed the crimes—followers of Charlie Manson. Oh my God. I *knew* he was creepy that night in Topanga, when I told him to go away. I wondered what became of Little Paul. I couldn't imagine that he would harm anyone.

Mondays through Fridays I'd wake up and hike down to the studio, eat breakfast and change from my nightgown and cowboy boots into one of my chic outfits from Charlie's Girls, or Betsy Johnson, or Norma Kamali—last year's samples I'd bought at The Clothing Mart. I'd drive my Volkswagen through Beverly Glen Canyon to the 101 Freeway and head south to downtown L.A. I'd tag watches, do some horoscopes and come home eight hours later. Things were stable and steady until October when one of the guys Tom sold some drugs to got busted. Understandably, Tom's friend told us we'd have to move. "I love you, man," he said to Tom. "But I don't want to go to jail."

I had mixed feelings about having to move again. The canyon was pretty, but it would be nice to return to civilization and have a bathroom I could use in the middle of the night. Tom decided on North Hollywood because it was so far away from "the scene of the crime." The small, two-bedroom house had linoleum floors. It came with a picnic table in the kitchen and an old brown couch. We brought our bed, books, clothes, pots and pans, a card table and two folding chairs. And the cat, who sulked on the front windowsill.

Tom's sister forwarded another draft notice. He couldn't afford to fly back to Milwaukee again, so I took him to the draft office in West Los Angeles and he re-registered. He started to starve himself again. His teeth hurt. Putting a hand on his stomach he said, "I feel like I have a hole in my inner-energy system." I took him to various doctors and clinics but they didn't find anything.

He stopped using his amplifier. He said the electricity went through his body and hurt. He stopped going in the car, the vibrations were too rough.

I felt so sad and hopeless. I heard about Gladys Jones, a psychic who had written *The Flowering Tree*, a metaphysical interpretation of reincarnation, four years earlier. I went to see her. Should I leave Los Angeles with Tom? If I refused to go would he stay with me or leave? Over the years I've gone to several psychics or had my cards read. None of their predictions came close to what ended up happening.

One bright spot, in that dismal fall of 1969 was a handwritten note I received from Henry Miller. Joe Gray had brought Henry to dinner several times and my father took a great series of photos that were published by Roger Jackson in 2000 as the *Henry Miller Portfolio, 18 unbound prints.* Either my father or Joe Gray gave Henry a copy of *Tender Bough.*

Oct. 30th 1969

> *I have tons of poetry thrown at me by aspiring young poets, and but I must confess I seldom find anything to my liking. But In these poems by Mary Lee ("Tender Bough") I am happy to say I find a simplicity, a beauty, a tenderness which is so lacking today and which is not old-fashioned, as some may think, but perpetually new and refreshing, inspiring to young and old alike.*

> *Henry Miller*

I was so happy to get his encouragement and find, when I got my first royalty check that the book was very popular at college bookstores.

Tom's health continued to decline. He announced one day, "No more tripping," and gave up psychedelics. But by now the harm was done. He spent most of his time sleeping on the couch.

Thanksgiving was a dismal affair. I found some fake turkey at the health food store, the only place Tom would let me shop for groceries. I made mashed potatoes and peas and sage dressing. We ate in the living room, at the card table, next to our little space heater, listening to Vivaldi's *Autumn.*

Tom decided some of my clothes were too sexy. He wanted me to be modest, stop bleaching my hair and shaving my legs. I relented on the hair, started parting it in the middle with the intention of letting it grow as long as it could. But I wouldn't stop shaving my legs, not while I wore miniskirts to work.

He asked me to model my clothes so he could choose which outfits were acceptable. He gave me thumbs up, or thumbs down. One of the dresses he wanted me to toss, because it was too sheer. Another was too tight. Or a skirt was too short. Tom let me keep a knit outfit, brown with white pinstripes. The skirt came to mid-thigh. The top had long sleeves, a V-neck, white collar and cuffs. A year later, wearing it to work at the perfume counter at Macy's in San Mateo, I got in trouble. When I bent over, customers could see I wasn't wearing a bra. I had to buy a camisole because, as a fledging feminist, I had thrown all my bras away.

On Friday, February 13, 1970, I got rear-ended, coming home from work on the crowded freeway. How much worse were things going to get? Tom and I had a sit-down one evening and made a plan: we would give our landlord notice, and leave within a month. We'd move to Dunsmuir, stopping in San Francisco where Tom would get his mouth fixed. We'd stay with Ann and Tracy—she rented a big basement of a mansion in Pacific Heights. Then once he recovered, we'd meet up with Tom's friend Mitchell and the three of us would live together—Tom writing songs, Mitchell and I writing poems.

I gave notice at work. My replacement's beautiful young daughter had disappeared and was never found. This horrific event led her to metaphysics. She and I had many deep discussions about destiny and alternative realities, that week we spent together.

What did my parents think of my plans? My mother had told me, "little bird, fly out of the nest." Well I'd flown all right. I was leaving behind everything I knew—people, places, jobs—heading north with a man I knew only a few months, a sickly songwriter with no legitimate income.

I was twenty years old, just a year younger than Mother when she married my father, on their third date. So maybe I got my impulsiveness from her. Years later Mother confessed that she and my dad were "sick with worry," when I left L.A. But I was of age. My life and my mistakes were my own.

My father built a wooden rack for the top of my Volkswagen, a sort of tray that would hold our mattress and bedding. The inside of the car was packed tight. My dad also built a cat carrier with a screen door for Bosco kitty. He had finally started to calm down. He let us pet him and would chase a toy mouse around the house instead of attacking us.

The night before we were scheduled to leave, I was just about to call the cat in for dinner when the doorbell rang. We always came in through the car port, so I hardly ever opened the front door. A man stood, clasping his hands.

"Do you have a Siamese cat with a red collar?"

"Yes," I answered.

"I'm sorry to tell you he's dead. On my lawn."

I felt like all my blood was being drained from my body. I began to melt. Tom, hearing voices, came out of the bedroom and caught me as my knees started to buckle. I went into the bathroom and sat on the edge of the tub and retched.

I could hear them talking. Bosco wasn't the only cat found dead in the neighborhood. Someone was poisoning cats. The man offered to dispose of Bosco, unless we wanted him back. Tom said no, we were moving tomorrow.

Tom closed the front door. He came into the bathroom, and sat beside me. He rubbed my back. I put my face in my hands and cried.

When I could talk I told Tom, "I don't want to stay here tonight. Let's go stay at my parents'. I'm ready to go now."

"All right," he agreed.

My mom made my favorite dinner, Indonesian chicken curry with lots of different condiments. In the morning I drove my little beige Volkswagen over the wooden bridge, my skinny, sickly songwriter beside me. Would I ever return to Southern California or would the rest of my life be lived elsewhere? Would I become a successful writer? Would Tom become a successful songwriter? Would we stay together?

A few weeks before our planned departure, Marc called. He'd transferred to Sonoma State University and was living in Sebastapol an hour north of San Francisco.

I told him we also were heading north. I felt the same way I always did about Marc: that we'd be together again, someday. I wasn't finished loving him.

I also learned from my sister that Linda moved to San Francisco with her gay lover. I wasn't surprised to find out Linda was a Lesbian. I remembered the night we spent in the cabin at Asilomar, how she asked me to take my top off, when she drew me. Enough time had passed since her friends' puppies had destroyed our house. I wasn't mad anymore. I was glad she had someone to love and looked forward to seeing her.

So I left L.A. with hope in my heart, that good things awaited me and Tom. I didn't want to believe the world was coming to an end, that California would fall into the sea. Tom would get his teeth fixed and become healthy. The Vietnam War would end soon and he would never have to starve himself again to get out of the draft.

In Dunsmuir I might get a cat, a sweet, loving cat. I had enough money from book royalties and savings to live three months. Plus, Crown agreed to have first right of refusal on my next book, which would be poems illustrated with my drawings.

I had poems to write and drawings to draw. I had a plan. I'd be okay.

Epilogue

My parents stayed married. They continued to work into their eighties. In 2010 my father broke his hip. Ten days later, on St. Patrick's Day, just two weeks shy of his ninety-fourth birthday, he died.

A month later our family had a private memorial at the house. We sat in the small living room and talked about Peter Gowland, his long, successful, happy life. Later, I wrote this poem.

LOSING MY FATHER

It was easy to say goodbye.

The man in the hospital bed
didn't look like my father. His arms
swollen and soft, not at all like the
brown muscular arms I remembered
all those years on the beach,
not even like the thin spotted arms
I saw last summer, skin like fabric
folded one too many times.
Childhood friends were coming to visit.
He said he was embarrassed for them
"To see me like this." "Oh," I joked,
just put on a shirt, your face looks great."
He smiled and when they arrived
he was wearing the soft cotton kimono he'd
purchased in Japan, forty-five years before.

The man in the hospital bed wore
a demeaning flimsy gown that had been
worn by others before him. Was it
burned with him in the crematory fire,
tossed in the trash, laundered and used
as rags or returned to the hospital
for some other wretched soul?

The urn containing his ashes is
an impersonal wooden box that
might once have held a bottle of whiskey,
or an Asian tea set. My mother strokes it
lovingly, the day the family gathers.
No one wants to open it so I
carry it into the kitchen, flip it over
like an animal about to be gutted, find
a Philips screwdriver in the drawer,
loosen the single silver screw,
slide open the lid to reveal a clear thick
plastic bag, tied with wire. Inside
mauve gray dust with shards of white.

I choose one of the modern, thin handled,
Brushed-stainless spoons my father liked,
not the black plastic-handled ones
my mother and I prefer. As I scoop him
into a yellow covered Chinese tea mug,
I restrain myself from
dipping in a finger for a taste.

Not that he would have minded.

This is not my father, I think,
yet I can feel him in the narrow kitchen
observing the procedure. I like that
he instilled in me a certain

detachment about the body, like
when he would extract a splinter from my finger.
He'd let me look through the jeweler's loop
before he passed a needle through the gas flame,
then painlessly remove the tiny sliver,
capable of causing so much pain.

His hands were steady and sure
not fluttering like injured birds
those last days, restlessly fiddling
with the heartbeat monitor
pinching his finger,
fluttering like dying birds.

The canyon where we scatter him
feels as if I can cup it in my hands.
It has lost the grandeur of my youth.
It's just a back yard, with very old trees.

Acknowledgements

In slightly different form, State Beach (2008), Europe on Five Dollars a Day (2009), and Daisies (2010) were recorded for *Valley Writers Read* on KVPR, Fresno, California. Thank you, Don Weaver and Franz Weinschenk for inspiring me to tell my stories.

Previously published poems include: from *Tender Bough*, "little girl grown," "the loneliness of morning's dawning rays," "I sat alone in contemplation," "reasoning means nothing," and "my skin's not black." From *Mountain Muse*, "Girl Child" and "Latimer Road." From *Women in Photography*, "Photographer's Kiss". From *Poetry on the Sand*, "The Slumber Party." I used "Hairy Lee" as a writing prompt in my book *Surprise Yourself! Fun Writing Exercises for Today's Kids*.

I want to thank Paula Karl and Izabel Ganz for reading the early drafts of this book.

I want to thank my writing teachers, and the other writers in their workshops, for being brutally honest, but always encouraging: Jack Grapes in Los Angeles, Peter Levitt when he was in Malibu, and Skye Alexander in Kerrville. And to Galway Kinnell, Sharon Olds, Brenda Hillman and Robert Hass for all I learned at the Squaw Valley Writers Conference.

I am grateful for poets who inspire me. I always look forward to the poems chosen by Ted Koozer for *American Life in Poetry*, and Garrison Keillor's for *Writer's Almanac* in my inbox. I love starting my day with a poem. I appreciate the Poetry Foundation and the National Endowment for the Arts for creating *Poetry Out Loud*, a national recitation competition for high school students. I applaud the Madera County Arts Council and Vision Academy of the Arts and other struggling non-profits who work so hard to bring visual, literary and performing arts to children.

Mary Lee Gowland

I thank my family and friends for sharing their lives with me and letting me write about them. I thank my husband John for his love and support. And of course I thank my mother and father for giving me good genes, an interesting early life, and for always encouraging me to express myself.

Notes on the Photos

Front Cover This photo was used in an ad, in the back of a photography magazine, with the caption: "Want to know more about the New, Compact GOWLANDFLEX with its selection of four different lenses, five film sizes and light-weight metal body? Write to my father, he makes them!" The street address, but no phone number was listed. Responders received brochures on cameras, books and posing guides. Sometimes amateur photographers just "dropped in." Many complained about getting lost and having to ask for directions (this was well before cell phones or gps) on the windy canyon roads. Luckily all the neighbors knew us and could explain how to find us.

"Natural Light" Mother pretends to read to me and Ann. In truth when we traveled in our trailer, I slept in the bunk bed. Plus, it's light outside, not night. But that's really how my sister sucked her thumb and I sucked two fingers and twirled my hair.

Chapter 1—Before I Was Born Both my parents were good dancers. I'm not sure who took the picture. I'm surprised my dad didn't insist on a clean background.

My first Christmas card, 1949. My father literally cut and pasted it up, then photographed the finished collage.

Chapter 2—Overland Avenue A vacant lot on one side of the building meant the exterior wall on that side could be used for signage. I believe the whole block was zoned commercial.

My father built my mother's desk, the planter along the wall, and the ceiling treatment, in his shop/garage.

Chapter 3—Rustic Canyon In this picture I'm five. I never had a good singing voice but I was good at lip-syncing and would do it at my parents' parties. Mother tried various outfits on me. At a different photo shoot, about a year later, my father sat at a table with his back to the camera, head in his hands while I lip-synced *Let Me Go Lover.*

We knew we could be photographed at any moment. Even though Mother has pin curls in her hair, she points her toe.

Chapter 4—Daisies Joe Gray, character actor and stunt double, was an important man in my life until his too-soon death in 1971. I loved to watch my father print pictures in his tidy darkroom.

Chapter 5—Glamour Girl Mother cutting my hair in the models' dressing room.

Chapter 6—Europe on Five Dollars a Day My dad staged this picture the day we picked up our car in Germany. He wanted to show how much it held: four people, five suitcases, three camera cases, two typewriters, my mother's and sister's gigantic purses and my father's bowler hat.

Chapter 7—Neighbors Susie and Teresa and I loved to dress up. The top picture of me and Susie, having a tea party, was sold many times as a stock photo and used in various ads. I have a copy of one from the back of an industrial magazine. A caption pointing to Susie says "and when I told my daddy how much money a stock oiler could save him on his punch press work—why, he offered me a job as his chief engineer." My caption says, "oh wow!"

Chapter 8—My Own Good Prisoner My father standing in the models' dressing room, late 1950s. He built the frame to hold some of his magazine covers and ads.

Chapter 9—The Awkward Years This is our Christmas card from 1962. Each of us, and Poncho, our dog, were photographed separately. Then the best of each were cut out, pasted up and reshot. This may explain why I'm so much bigger than my sister.

Chapter 10—State Beach This photo is credited to Lou Jacobs who was a fellow photographer and good friend of my parents.

Chapter 11—God and Grandmothers My father's mother wrote poetry and stories and got bit parts in films. The photo my dad took for her *Snake Pit* audition is too scary to include here. She got the part as one of the mental patients in the 1948 drama starring Olivia de Haviland. Several years later she was committed to the state mental hospital in Camarillo and received shock treatments for schizophrenia.

Chapter 12—The Bay Theater A test shot to set the lights for a Black Velvet ad. Professional models charged by the hour so my father got everything set up the day before, using me and or/my sister as stand-ins. I'm fifteen, with braces, one false eyelash falling off and a bathing suit tan line; Ann, at twenty-one is just plain gorgeous. But she had no interest in modeling.

Chapter 13—I Become a Dancer Bluth Brothers Theater in Culver City was a converted supermarket where we performed *Blithe Spirit,* the summer of 1965.

Chapter 14—1966 The head shot for the portfolio I took to the Mary Webb Davis modeling agency in Hollywood.

Chapter 15—I Become a Poet I'm only two in this picture, but I remember the white feather quill, and the bottle of black India ink, with its rubber-stopper top.

Chapter 16—Mother Moves Out I'm sitting on a piece of fencing we dragged down to the beach, along with an antique chair and all the usual camera equipment.

Chapter 17—Marc, Marijuana & Movies I finally make the cover of a magazine!

Chapter 18—Topanga When I moved away from home I didn't take a camera with me. I have no pictures of our little white house next to the Malibu Feed Bin or the people I knew. Mother took this picture of me in the creek in front of their house, but it reminds me of the Topanga creek and "the snake pit" behind our house.

Chapter 19—Tom I did lots of pencil and pen-and-ink drawings when I lived with Tom. This picture shows me holding a duck's head. Somehow Linda's friend's puppies killed a duck and scattered it all over the living room.

Chapter 20—Tender Bough This was the first time Mother got credit. When I saw all our names together, I felt embarrassed and didn't want people to know my parents had taken the pictures, so I dropped my last name. I took it back after my divorce in 1977 and did not change it when I married John Busch in 1992.

Epilogue—Photo of me and my father taken by Cecil Ballerino.